D0116840

THE CALIFORNIA DIRECTORY OF
FINE WINERIES

SIXTH EDITION

THE CALIFORNIA DIRECTORY OF
FineWineries

K. REKA BADGER, CHERYL CRABTREE, AND MARTY OLMSTEAD, WRITERS

ROBERT HOLMES, PHOTOGRAPHER

TOM SILBERKLEIT, EDITOR AND PUBLISHER

WINE HOUSE PRESS

CONTENTS

INTRODUCTION

Whether you are a visitor or a native seeking the ultimate chalice of nectar from the grape, navigating Northern California's wine country can be intimidating. Hundreds of wineries —from glamorous estates to converted barns, from nationally recognized labels to hidden gems— are found throughout Napa, Sonoma, and Mendocino. The challenge is deciding where to go and how to plan a trip. This book will be your indispensable traveling companion.

The sixty-eight wineries in this fully updated, sixth edition of *The California Directory of Fine Wineries* are known for producing some of the world's most admired wines. From the moment you walk in the door of these wineries, you will be greeted like a guest and invited to sample at a relaxing, leisurely tempo. Although the quality of the winemaker's art is of paramount importance, the wineries are also notable as tourist destinations. Many boast award-winning contemporary architecture, while others are housed in lovingly preserved historical structures. Some have galleries featuring museum-quality artwork by local and international artists or exhibits focusing on the region's past and the history of winemaking. You will also enjoy taking informative behind-the-scenes tours, exploring inspirational gardens, and participating in celebrated culinary programs. With a bit of advance planning, you can arrange to take part in a barrel sampling, a blending seminar, or a grape stomping.

As you explore this magnificent region, you'll encounter some of California's most appealing scenery and attractions—mountain ranges, rugged coastline, pastures with majestic oak trees, abundant parkland, renowned spas, and historic towns. Use the information in this book to plan your trip, and be sure to stop along the way and take in the sights. You have my promise that traveling to your destination will be as pleasurable as the wine tasted upon your welcome.

—Tom Silberkleit
Editor and Publisher
Wine House Press
Sonoma, California

THE ETIQUETTE OF WINE TASTING

Most of the wineries profiled in this book offer amenities ranging from lush gardens to art exhibitions, but their main attraction is the tasting room. This is where winery employees get a chance to share their products and knowledge with consumers, in hopes of establishing a lifelong relationship. They are there to please.

Yet, for some visitors, the ritual of tasting fine wines can be intimidating. Perhaps it's because swirling wine and using a spit bucket seem to be unnatural acts. But with a few tips, even a first-time taster can enjoy the experience. After all, the point of tasting is to enhance your knowledge by learning the differences among varieties of wines, styles of winemaking, and appellations.

A list of available wines is usually posted, beginning with whites and ending with the heaviest reds or, if available, dessert wines. Look for the tasting notes, which are typically set out on the counter; refer to them as you taste each wine. A number of wineries charge a tasting fee for four or five wines of your choosing or for a "flight" — most often several preselected wines. In any event, the tasting process is the same.

After you are served, hold the stem of the glass with your thumb and as many fingers as you need to maintain control. Lift the glass up to the light and note the color and intensity of the wine. Good wines tend to be bright, with the color fading near the rim. Next, gently swirl the wine in the glass. Observe how much of the wine adheres to the sides of the glass. If lines — called legs — are visible, the wine is viscous, indicating body or weight as well as a high alcohol content. Now, tip the glass to about a 45-degree angle, take a short sniff, and concentrate on the aromas. Swirl the wine again to aerate it, releasing additional aromas. Take another sniff and see if the "bouquet" reminds you of anything — rose petals, citrus fruit, or a freshly ironed pillowcase, for example — that will help you identify the aroma.

Finally, take a sip and swirl the wine around your tongue, letting your taste buds pick up all the flavors. The wine may remind you of honey or cherries or mint — as with the "nosing," try to make as many associations as you can. Then spit the wine into the bucket on the counter. Afterward, notice how long the flavor stays in your mouth; a long finish is the ideal. If you don't want another taste, just pour the wine remaining in your glass into the bucket and move on. Remember, the more you spit or pour out, the more wines you will enjoy sampling.

The next level of wine tasting involves guided tastings and food-and-wine pairings. In these sessions, a few cheeses or a series of appetizers are paired with a flight of wines, usually a selection of three red or three white wines presented in the recommended order of tasting. The server will explain what goes with what.

If you still feel self-conscious, practice at home. Once you are in a real tasting room, you'll be better able to focus on the wine itself. That's the real payoff, because once you learn what you like and why you like it, you'll be able to recognize wines in a similar vein anywhere in the world.

WHAT IS AN APPELLATION?

The word *appellation* is often used to refer to the geographical area where wine grapes were grown. If the appellation is named on the bottle label, it means that at least 85 percent of the wine is from that area.

The terms "appellation of origin" and "American Viticultural Area" (AVA) are frequently used interchangeably in casual conversation, but they are not synonymous. In the United States, appellations follow geopolitical borders, such as state and county lines, rather than geographic boundaries. AVAs are defined by such natural features as soil types, climate, and topography.

The U.S. Alcohol and Tobacco Tax and Trade Bureau is the arbiter of what does and does not qualify as an AVA. A winery or other interested party that wants a particular area to qualify as an official AVA must supply proof that it has enough specific attributes to distinguish it significantly from its neighbors.

Why do winemakers care? Because it is far more prestigious—and informative—to label a wine with an appellation such as Sonoma County, Napa Valley, or Russian River Valley than with the more generic California, which means the grapes could have come from the Central Valley or anywhere else in the state. Moreover, informed consumers learn that a Chardonnay from the Alexander Valley, for instance, is apt to smell and taste different from one originating in the Russian River Valley. A winery may be located in one appellation but use grapes from another to make a particular wine. In this case, the appellation on the label would indicate the source of the grapes rather than the physical location of the winery.

The following are the appellations in Napa, Sonoma, and Mendocino:

NAPA	SONOMA	MENDOCINO
Atlas Peak	Alexander Valley	Anderson Valley
Calistoga	Bennett Valley	Cole Ranch
Chiles Valley	Chalk Hill	Covelo
Coombsville	Dry Creek Valley	Dos Rios
Diamond Mountain District	Fort Ross–Seaview	McDowell Valley
Howell Mountain	Green Valley	Mendocino
Los Carneros	Knights Valley	Mendocino Ridge
Mount Veeder	Los Carneros	North Coast
Napa Valley	North Coast	Potter Valley
North Coast	Northern Sonoma	Redwood Valley
Oak Knoll District	Rockpile	Sanel Valley (pending)
Oakville	Russian River Valley	Ukiah Valley (pending)
Rutherford	Sonoma Coast	Yorkville Highlands
Spring Mountain District	Sonoma Mountain	
St. Helena	Sonoma Valley	
Stags Leap District		
Wild Horse Valley		
Yountville		

Napa

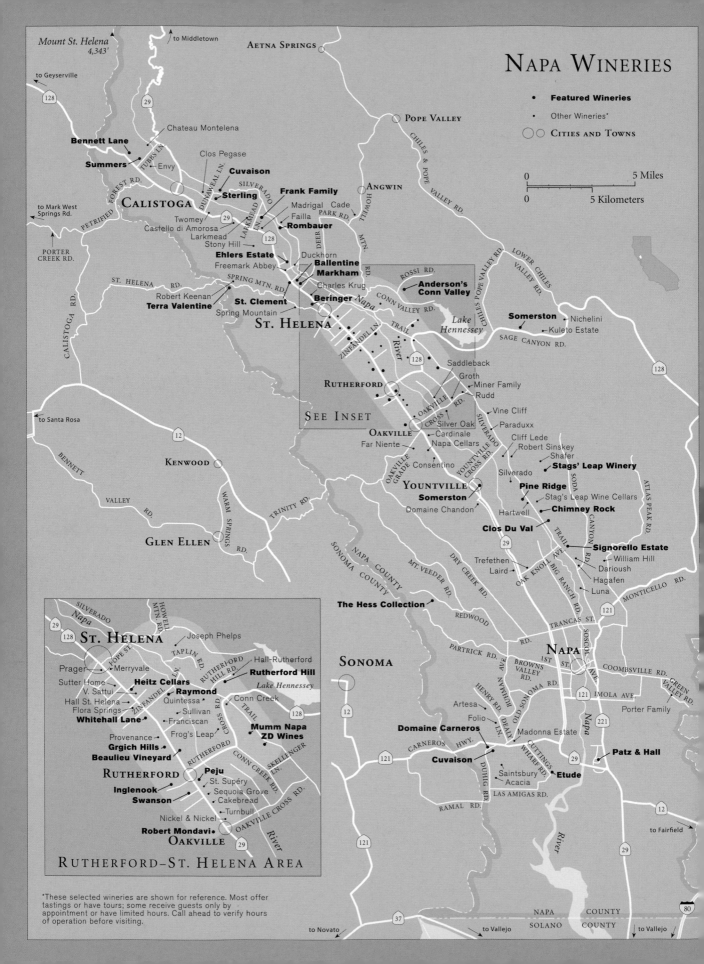

NAPA WINERIES

- ● **Featured Wineries**
- • Other Wineries*
- ◯ ◯ **CITIES AND TOWNS**

0 ————— 5 Miles
0 ————— 5 Kilometers

Mount St. Helena
4,343'

to Middletown

AETNA SPRINGS

to Geyserville

128

29

Chateau Montelena

Bennett Lane

Clos Pegase

POPE VALLEY

Summers

Envy
TUBBS LN.

Cuvaison

Sterling

Frank Family

ANGWIN

PETRIFIED FOREST RD.

DUNAWEAL LN.

SILVERADO

Madrigal Cade
Failla

PARK RD.

to Mark West
Springs Rd.

CALISTOGA

Twomey
Castello di Amorosa
Larkmead
Stony Hill

29

LARKMEAD LN.

128

Rombauer

DEER

HOWELL MTN. RD.

CHILES & POPE VALLEY RD.

PORTER
CREEK RD.

ST. HELENA RD.

SPRING MTN. RD.

Ehlers Estate
Freemark Abbey

Ballentine
Markham

Duckhorn

ROSSI RD.

LOWER CHILES VALLEY RD.

Robert Keenan

Charles Krug

**Anderson's
Conn Valley**

128

Terra Valentine

St. Clement
Spring Mountain

Beringer

CONN VALLEY RD.

Lake
Hennessey

Somerston
• Nichelini

CALISTOGA RD.

ST. HELENA

Napa

TRAIL

• Kuleto Estate

SAGE CANYON RD.

to Santa Rosa

ZINFANDEL LN.

River

128

Saddleback

Groth

128

RUTHERFORD

• Miner Family
Rudd

12

KENWOOD

BENNETT

SEE INSET

OAKVILLE CROSS RD.

Silver Oak
Cardinale
Napa Cellars

Vine Cliff

Paraduxx

Cliff Lede
Robert Sinskey
Shafer

SILVERADO TRAIL

128

VALLEY

WARM SPRINGS RD.

TRINITY RD.

OAKVILLE

Far Niente

OAKVILLE GRADE

Consentino

Stags' Leap Winery

Silverado

GLEN ELLEN

YOUNTVILLE CROSS RD.

Pine Ridge

SODA CANYON RD.

ATLAS PEAK RD.

YOUNTVILLE

Somerston

Domaine Chandon

Stag's Leap Wine Cellars

Chimney Rock

Hartwell

Clos Du Val

SONOMA COUNTY

NAPA COUNTY

MT. VEEDER RD.

DRY CREEK RD.

29

Trefethen
Laird

OAK KNOLL AVE.

BIG RANCH RD.

Signorello Estate
• William Hill

Darioush

Hagafen

Luna

MONTICELLO RD.

REDWOOD

The Hess Collection

121

TRANCAS ST.

PARTRICK RD.

BROWNS VALLEY RD.

SOSCOL AVE.

1ST ST.

NAPA

COOMBSVILLE RD.

GREEN VALLEY RD.

12

SONOMA

HENRY RD.

DEALY LN.

OLD SONOMA RD.

121 IMOLA AVE.

Porter Family

RUTHERFORD–ST. HELENA AREA

SILVERADO

Napa

29

128

ST. HELENA

Joseph Phelps

HOWELL MTN. RD.

Prager

POPE ST.

Merryvale

TAPLIN RD.

Hall-Rutherford

Sutter Home

Heitz Cellars

V. Sattui

Raymond

RUTHERFORD HILL RD.

Rutherford Hill

Lake Hennessey

Hall St. Helena
Flora Springs

ZINFANDEL LN.

Quintessa

Conn Creek

Whitehall Lane

Sullivan
Franciscan

CONN CREEK RD.

Frog's Leap

128

**Mumm Napa
ZD Wines**

Artesa
Folio

221

Madonna Estate

Provenance

Grgich Hills
Beaulieu Vineyard

RUTHERFORD

CROSS RD.

SKELLENGER LN.

Domaine Carneros

Peju

RUTHERFORD

St. Supéry

CARNEROS HWY.

DUHIG RD.

CUTTINGS WHARF RD.

29

Patz & Hall

Inglenook

Sequoia Grove

Cuvaison

Swanson

Cakebread

Saintsbury
Acacia

Etude

Turnbull

Nickel & Nickel

OAKVILLE CROSS RD.

LAS AMIGAS RD.

Robert Mondavi

River

OAKVILLE

29

121

RAMAL RD.

12

to Fairfield

37

to Novato

121

NAPA   COUNTY
SOLANO   COUNTY

80

to Vallejo

to Vallejo

*These selected wineries are shown for reference. Most offer
tastings or have tours; some receive guests only by
appointment or have limited hours. Call ahead to verify hours
of operation before visiting.

The Napa Valley, jam-packed with hundreds of premium wineries and thousands of acres of coveted vineyards, has earned its position as the country's number one winemaking region. From its southern tip at San Pablo Bay, about an hour's drive from San Francisco, this picture-perfect patchwork of agriculture extends thirty miles north to the dramatic Palisades that tower above Calistoga. The narrow, scenic valley is defined on the east by a series of  hills known as the Vaca Range and on the west by the rugged peaks of the Mayacamas Range, including the steep forested slopes of Mount Veeder. St. Helena, where upscale stores and chic boutiques line the historic Main Street, is the jewel in the region's crown. At the southern end of the valley, the city of Napa has experienced a boom in recent years, with a plethora of restaurants and attractions such as the vibrant Oxbow Public Market. The mostly two-lane Highway 29 links these and smaller towns that welcome visitors with a variety of spas, restaurants, and bed-and-breakfast inns.

For an unforgettable impression, book a hot-air balloon ride or simply drive up the winding Oakville Grade and pull over at the top for a view worthy of a magazine cover.

ANDERSON'S CONN VALLEY VINEYARDS

Less than a ten-minute drive from bustling downtown St. Helena, Anderson's Conn Valley Vineyards occupies a niche in a valley within a valley. The location is so remote that most drivers along Conn Valley Road aren't even aware the winery exists. Out here, you could hear a pin drop, except during the busy harvest season that begins in late summer.

Anderson's Conn Valley Vineyards was founded in 1983 by Gus and Todd Anderson along with their wives, Phyllis and Dana. Gus Anderson spearheaded the lengthy search for vineyard property in Napa Valley. He had the advantage of realizing Napa's tremendous potential before the region became widely known (in the wake of the famous 1976 Paris tasting that put Napa on the world wine map) and before land in the wine country became prohibitively expensive.

Joseph Heitz and Joseph Phelps had already established wineries in the neighborhood by the time the Andersons found their dream site, forty acres in the eastern part of the St. Helena American Viticultural Area near the base of Howell Mountain. Unfortunately, the acreage was not for sale; it would take fifteen months of negotiations to secure the property.

Then the real work of establishing a winery operation began, and for the most part, it has all been done by the Andersons. Todd Anderson left his profession as a geophysicist to pound posts, hammer nails, and install twenty-six and a half acres of prime vineyards. That was just the beginning. While the vines matured, the Andersons created a fifteen-acre-foot reservoir and built the winery, the residence, and a modest cave system.

The family did hire professionals with the necessary heavy-duty equipment to expand the caves by 8,000 square feet. Completed in 2001, the 9,000-square-foot caves feature a warren of narrow pathways beneath the hillside. Deep in the caverns, one wall has been pushed out to make way for tables and chairs where visitors can sample the wines. In clement weather, tastings are often held on the far side of the caves, with seating beneath market umbrellas at tables that overlook the reservoir.

Tours and tastings are led by Todd Anderson, who now operates Anderson's Conn Valley Vineyards. A great advantage to touring a family winery is the chance to get to know the people behind the wines and to linger long enough to ask questions that might never get answered during a large group tour at one of Napa's big and better-known wineries located along either Highway 29 or the Silverado Trail.

ANDERSON'S CONN VALLEY VINEYARDS
680 Rossi Rd.
St. Helena, CA 94574
707-963-8600
800-946-3497
info@connvalleyvineyards.com
www.connvalleyvineyards.com

OWNERS: Anderson family.

LOCATION: 3.3 miles east of Silverado Trail via Howell Mountain Rd. and Conn Valley Rd.

APPELLATION: Napa Valley.

HOURS: 9 A.M.–5 P.M. Monday–Friday; 10 A.M.–2 P.M. Saturday–Sunday.

TASTINGS: By appointment. $25 for current release tasting, $45 for barrel cave tasting.

TOURS: By appointment. 10 A.M., 12 P.M., and 2 P.M., Monday–Friday; 10 A.M., 12 P.M., and 2 P.M., Saturday and Sunday.

THE WINES: Cabernet Sauvignon, Chardonnay, Pinot Noir, Sauvignon Blanc.

SPECIALTIES: Cabernet Sauvignon, Bordeaux blends.

WINEMAKER: Todd Anderson.

ANNUAL PRODUCTION: 8,500 cases.

OF SPECIAL NOTE: Barrel tasting, lunch, and other special events are available at varying prices by advance arrangement. Tours and tastings are held in extensive winery caves.

NEARBY ATTRACTIONS: Bothe-Napa State Park (hiking, picnicking, horseback riding, swimming Memorial Day–Labor Day); Silverado Museum (Robert Louis Stevenson memorabilia).

BALLENTINE VINEYARDS

BALLENTINE VINEYARDS
2820 St. Helena Hwy. North
St. Helena, CA 94574
707-963-7919
info@ballentinevineyards.
com
www.ballentinevineyards.
com

OWNERS: Van and Betty
Ballentine.

LOCATION: 3 miles north of
St. Helena on east side of St.
Helena Hwy.

APPELLATIONS: St. Helena,
Napa Valley.

HOURS: 10 A.M.–5 P.M. daily.

TASTINGS: $5 for 4 wines;
$10 for 4 reserve wines.
Reservations required.

TOURS: By appointment.

THE WINES: Cabernet Franc,
Cabernet Sauvignon,
Chardonnay, Chenin Blanc,
Malvasia Bianca, Merlot,
Petit Verdot, Petite Sirah,
Syrah, Zinfandel.

SPECIALTIES: Cabernet Franc,
Chardonnay, Malvasia
Bianca Frizzante, Petit
Verdot, Petite Sirah.

WINEMAKER: Bruce Devlin.

ANNUAL PRODUCTION:
10,000 cases.

OF SPECIAL NOTE: Reserve
Chardonnay and Reserve
Cabernet Sauvignon sold in
tasting room only. Zinfandel
Port-style wine available.

NEARBY ATTRACTIONS: Bothe-
Napa State Park (hiking,
picnicking, horseback
riding, swimming Memorial
Day–Labor Day); Bale Grist
Mill State Historic park
(water-powered mill circa
1846); Culinary Institute
of America at Greystone
(cooking demonstrations);
Silverado Museum
(Robert Louis Stevenson
memorabilia).

Longtime locals Betty and Van Ballentine grew up in the wine business. In fact, their combined family histories represent more than a century of Napa Valley winemaking. The couple met as teenagers and married more than fifty years ago. Since then, they have continued to grow grapes and make wine just as their parents and grandparents did, offering visitors classic varieties and old-world hospitality.

Born in Italy, Betty's grandfather immigrated to California in 1884 and helped plant the vineyards at what would become Korbel Champagne Cellars. In 1906 he moved to Calistoga, planted his own sixty-acre vineyard, and built a winery. After Betty's grandfather died, her father and uncle operated the winery until closing its doors in 1963. The old vineyard near Calistoga lives on under the care of the Ballentines and supplies extraordinary fruit for several wines, including the reserve Zinfandel.

Van, an experienced viticulturist, spent his formative years working in the St. Helena–area vineyard and winery his father purchased in 1922. The elder Ballentine dubbed his brand Deer Park, after the family farm in Ireland. In 1944 Van and his father acquired twenty-five acres just north of St. Helena. Currently planted to Merlot, Syrah, and Malvasia Bianca, the land is called Betty's Vineyard. It is home to Ballentine Vineyards, as well as to Betty and Van, who live in a one-hundred-year-old farmhouse beside the driveway.

After his father's winery closed in 1959, Van continued to farm wine grapes. He sold the fruit to local producers, such as Caymus Vineyards and Robert Mondavi Winery, and spent a half-dozen years managing the vineyards at Christian Brothers Winery. Van yearned to return to winemaking, so in 1992 he and Betty revived the Deer Park winery and launched Ballentine Vineyards. Three years later, they built a solar-powered winery with an attached tasting room opposite Betty's Vineyard. Remodeled in 2009, the intimate tasting room blooms with tropical greenery, and friendly staff members offer a warm greeting. Espresso-stained cabinetry and black granite countertops complement the blue-gray flagstone flooring and cut crystal counter buckets.

The Ballentines source their fruit from three estate vineyards, including the sixteen-acre Crystal Springs Vineyard, near Howell Mountain. They purchased the land in 1949 and installed Petite Sirah and Petit Verdot. Syrah planted in 1960 at Crystal Springs Vineyard remains the oldest Syrah in Napa Valley. In 2002 the Ballentines named Bruce Devlin as their winemaker, but Van continues to tend the vineyards and keep a close eye on wines bottled under the family name.

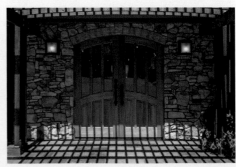

BEAULIEU VINEYARD

French immigrant and winemaker Georges de Latour and his wife, Fernande, bought their first Rutherford ranch in 1900. "Beau lieu!" Fernande declared when she saw the ranch, deeming it a "beautiful place." Thus, Beaulieu Vineyard, also known simply as BV, was named. Among the first to recognize Rutherford's potential for yielding stellar Cabernet Sauvignon, Georges de Latour was determined to craft wine to rival the French. By 1909 he had expanded his vineyard and established a nursery for cultivating phylloxera-resistant rootstock. For a time, the nursery supplied a half-million grafted vines annually to California vineyards.

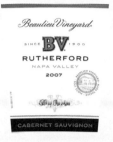

In 1938 de Latour hired André Tchelistcheff, who declared Sauvignon worthy of flagship he introduced a number of including controlling heat during and protect delicate fruit flavors, than American, oak barrels for fabled, Russian-born enologist the 1936 Private Reserve Cabernet status. With de Latour's blessing, practices now considered standard, fermentation to keep wines cool and barrel aging in French, rather the addition of more nuanced components. As a result, BV's Private Reserve became Napa Valley's first "cult Cab" and continues to rank among the region's most widely collected wines.

Housed in a Boston ivy–clad complex built in three different centuries, the gray stone and concrete winery faces the visitor center across a parking lot studded with sycamores and oaks. Guests follow a path edged with manicured boxwood and roses to reach the center, a two-story, hexagonal building with stone exterior. Upon entering, they are immediately handed a complimentary glass of wine in homage to Mrs. de Latour's peerless hospitality. Natural light spills from above, bathing the redwood interior. A curved staircase leads down an open well to the Club Room, where visitors who reserve ahead can enjoy a seated tasting.

A few steps from the visitor center is the Reserve Room, dedicated to the winery's flagship Georges de Latour Private Reserve Cabernet Sauvignon. At a softly lit marble-topped bar, visitors can taste winery exclusives and library wines, or purchase vintages of the Private Reserve going back to 1970. Fieldstone walls mimic those of BV's core winery, built in 1885. In a cozy side room, a glass-topped table displays bottles representing singular moments in the winery's history, including a release of Pure Altar Wine vinified during Prohibition. A brilliant businessman, de Latour prospered despite grape shortages, insect infestations, and Prohibition. More than a century later, Beaulieu Vineyard reigns as a leader in the production of acclaimed Cabernet Sauvignon and is among the longest continually operating wineries in Napa Valley.

BEAULIEU VINEYARD
1960 St. Helena Hwy.
Rutherford, CA 94573
800-264-6918, ext. 5233
707-967-5233
visitingbv@bvwines.com
www.bvwines.com

OWNER: Diageo Chateau and Estate Wines.

LOCATION: About 3 miles south of St. Helena.

APPELLATION: Rutherford.

HOURS: 10 A.M.–5 P.M. daily.

TASTINGS: Maestro Wine Tasting, $15 for choice of 4 wines from winery-only Maestro series. Cabernet Tasting, $20 for vineyard and clonal selections exclusive to BV. Reserve Tasting, $30 for current and library Georges de Latour Private Reserve Cabernet Sauvignon. Retrospective Reserve Tasting, $50 for a flight of 4 Georges de Latour Private Reserve Cabernet Sauvignon; reservations required.

TOURS: Historic Tour and Barrel Tasting ($20) includes tour of the 1885 winery and BV museum; reservations required.

THE WINES: Cabernet Sauvignon, Chardonnay, Merlot, Sauvignon Blanc.

SPECIALTIES: Rutherford Cabernet Sauvignon, Georges de Latour Private Reserve Cabernet Sauvignon.

WINEMAKER: Jeffrey Stambor.

ANNUAL PRODUCTION: 300,000 cases.

OF SPECIAL NOTE: 15 small-lot wines available in tasting room only. Clone series (Cabernet Sauvignon) and Reserve Tapestry series (Bordeaux blends) available in the Reserve Room.

NEARBY ATTRACTION: Culinary Institute of America at Greystone (cooking demonstrations).

BENNETT LANE WINERY

BENNETT LANE WINERY
3340 Hwy. 128
Calistoga, CA 94515
877-629-6272
info@bennettlane.com
www.bennettlane.com

OWNERS: Randy and
Lisa Lynch.

LOCATION: About 2 miles
north of Calistoga.

APPELLATION: Napa Valley.

HOURS: 10 A.M.–5:30 P.M.
daily.

TASTINGS: $15 for 4 wines;
$40 for Reserve Cabernet
Sauvignon.

TOURS: Daily, by
appointment.

THE WINES: Cabernet
Sauvignon, Chardonnay,
Maximus (red blend),
White Maximus
(white blend).

SPECIALTIES: Cabernet
Sauvignon, Maximus.

WINEMAKER: Grant
Hermann.

ANNUAL PRODUCTION:
12,000 cases.

OF SPECIAL NOTE: Varietals
Fruit Flavor Custom
Blend Experience, by
appointment ($200 per
person) and including a
tour and tasting of current
releases with cheese
pairing, allows visitors to
create and bottle their own
wine. Reserve Chardonnay
and Syrah available
only at tasting room.
Annual events include
Cabernet Release Weekend
(February).

NEARBY ATTRACTIONS:
Old Faithful Geyser of
California; Robert Louis
Stevenson State Park
(hiking).

Far from the din and traffic of central Napa Valley, Bennett Lane Winery lures adventure-some Cabernet Sauvignon lovers to the northernmost wedge of the valley, where the Vaca Range meets the Mayacamas Range. This sequestered setting just north of the town of Calistoga features dramatic views of Mount St. Helena and the Palisades, which provide an ideal backdrop for Bennett Lane's handcrafted, small-lot wines. Bennett Lane's signature wine is named Maximus, after the second-century Roman emperor Magnus Maximus, a noted vinophile of his day. The exact percentages of varietals that go into the Maximus wines vary somewhat from vintage to vintage. The Maximus Red Feasting Wine is a typical blend, made primarily from Cabernet Sauvignon, with the addition of 20 percent or so Merlot, as well as a small amount of Malbec and, sometimes, Petit Verdot. At Bennett Lane, blending is the name of the game, and tasters eager to learn more about this elusive art are invited to take part in a special program whereby they taste and combine a selection of varietals to create their own Maximus blend.

Visitors to the Mediterranean-style winery are welcomed into a tasting room painted in warm tones of brown and Tuscan gold. Enhancements added during a 2012 remodel include upholstered armchairs for relaxing and a Brazilian granite tasting bar. In order to provide a tasting experience that is enjoyable and educational, as well as interactive, iPads have been mounted along the bar. Here visitors can access a dynamic application that describes Bennett Lane wines and their source vineyards. The app also delivers the latest reviews, detailed tasting notes, and tempting recipes to pair with the wines. The iPads make it easy for tasters to share their wine discoveries with friends via social media, or enter and e-mail their tasting notes to fellow wine lovers.

Owners Randy and Lisa Lynch were relative newcomers to the world of wine in 2003, when they purchased what had once been a custom crush facility. Originally, they had been looking for a second home with vineyard land, and soon after purchasing a residence in Calistoga, they bought the Bennett Lane property. The Lynches were encouraged by critical praise for their wines, whose fruit now comes from highly acclaimed sources in Napa Valley. These vineyards are dotted throughout the valley, from Yountville in the south to Randy Lynch's vineyard in Calistoga in the north. Lynch's goal is to create wines that are both approachable and complex, what he calls "the best of both worlds, meaning you can drink them today, but they are structured enough to cellar for several years."

BERINGER VINEYARDS

With the 1883 Rhine House, hand-carved aging tunnels, and a heritage dating to 1876, Beringer Vineyards is steeped in history like few other wineries in California. Among the oldest continuously operating wineries in Napa Valley, it combines age-old traditions with up-to-date technology to create a wide range of award-winning wines.

It was German know-how that set the Beringer brothers on the path to glory. Jacob and Frederick Beringer emigrated from Mainz, Germany, to the United States in the 1860s. Jacob, having worked in cellars in Germany, was intrigued when he heard that the California climate was ideal for growing the varietal grapes that flourished in Europe's winemaking regions. Leaving Frederick in New York, he traveled west in 1870 to discover that Napa Valley's rocky, well-drained soils were similar to those in his native Rhine Valley. Five years later, he bought land with Frederick and began excavating the hillsides to create tunnels for aging his wines. The brothers founded Beringer Vineyards in 1876. During the building of the caves and winery, Jacob lived in an 1848 farmhouse that today is known as the Hudson House. The meticulously restored and expanded structure now serves as Beringer Vineyards' Culinary Arts Center.

But the star attraction on the lavishly landscaped grounds is unquestionably the seventeen-room Rhine House, which Frederick modeled after his ancestral home in Germany. The redwood, brick, and stucco mansion is painted in the original Tudor color scheme of earth tones, and slate covers the gabled roof and exterior. The interior of the Rhine House is graced with myriad gems of craftsmanship such as Belgian art nouveau–style stained-glass windows.

Beringer Vineyards was the first winery in Napa Valley to give public tours and continues the tradition today by offering two tours, each covering the winery and its fascinating history. An introductory tour takes visitors to the cellars and hand-dug aging tunnels in the Old Stone Winery, where they can also enjoy wine tasting. A longer, more in-depth tour, the Taste of Beringer, includes the demonstration vineyard, where visitors will learn about grape growing, and a wine tasting in the Rhine House, where they will hear about Beringer's winemaking techniques and experience firsthand how to taste wine like a professional.

BERINGER VINEYARDS
2000 Main St.
St. Helena, CA 94574
866-708-9463
www.beringer.com

OWNER: Treasury Wine Estates.

LOCATION: On Hwy. 29 about .5 mile north of St. Helena.

APPELLATION: Napa Valley.

HOURS: 10 A.M.–5 P.M. daily in winter; until 6 P.M. in summer.

TASTINGS AND TOURS: Various options are available. Check www.beringer.com for information and reservations.

THE WINES: Cabernet Sauvignon, Chardonnay, Merlot, Pinot Noir, Sauvignon Blanc.

SPECIALTIES: Private Reserve Cabernet Sauvignon, single-vineyard Cabernet Sauvignon, Private Reserve Chardonnay.

WINEMAKER: Laurie Hook.

ANNUAL PRODUCTION: Unavailable.

OF SPECIAL NOTE: Tour includes visit to barrel storage caves hand-chiseled in late 1800s.

NEARBY ATTRACTIONS: Bothe-Napa State Park (hiking, picnicking, horseback riding, swimming Memorial Day–Labor Day); Silverado Museum (Robert Louis Stevenson memorabilia).

CHIMNEY ROCK WINERY

CHIMNEY ROCK WINERY
5350 Silverado Trail
Napa, CA 94558
800-257-2641
707-257-2641
info@chimneyrock.com
www.chimneyrock.com

OWNERS: Terlato family.

LOCATION: 3 miles south
of Yountville.

APPELLATION: Stags Leap
District.

HOURS: 10 A.M.–5 P.M. daily.

TASTINGS: $20–$35 for 3
or 4 wines; from $30 for
private tastings.

TOURS: Estate tour and
tasting ($55), barrel tasting
($85), and vineyard tour
and luncheon ($90) offered
daily by appointment.

THE WINES: Cabernet Franc,
Cabernet Sauvignon, Mer-
lot, Petit Verdot, Sauvignon
Blanc, Sauvignon Gris.

SPECIALTIES: 100 percent
estate-grown single-
vineyard Stags Leap District
Cabernet Sauvignons,
Elevage (red Bordeaux
blend), Elevage Blanc (white
Bordeaux blend).

WINEMAKER:
Elizabeth Vianna.

ANNUAL PRODUCTION:
30,000 cases.

OF SPECIAL NOTE: Rotating
display of artworks. Annual
Vineyard to Vintner event
(April) by Stags Leap
District winegrowers.
Winery is pet friendly.

NEARBY ATTRACTIONS: Napa
Valley Museum (winemak-
ing displays, art exhibits);
Napa Valley Opera House
(live performances in historic building).

A quarter mile past the elegant wrought iron gates of Chimney Rock Winery, the broad face of the winery gleams beyond converging rows of meticulously farmed Cabernet Sauvignon vines. Whitewashed walls, arched doorways, and soaring gables define and distinguish the eye-catching architecture. Marking the eastern border of the Stags Leap District, the oak-studded Vaca Range is a dramatic backdrop for the winery and harbors the volcanic formation that gave the winery its name.

In 1980 Sheldon "Hack" Wilson, after multiple business successes, turned his talents and resources to making great wines. He, along with his wife, Stella, bought a pristine 185-acre property just south of Yountville and promptly planted 74 acres of Cabernet Sauvignon. By 1990 the couple had completed the tasting room and adjacent winery in the Cape Dutch style of Stella's native South Africa. For the winery's facade, the Wilsons commissioned a decorative frieze that depicts Ganymede — cupbearer to the mythical gods of ancient Greece — which gives the building a timeless, old-world feel. An avid gardener and horticulturist, Stella designed and planted elaborate beds surrounding both their home and the winery. The abundant gardens continue to flourish today.

In 2000 the Wilsons partnered with the Terlato family, whose participation in the wine industry had spanned more than fifty years and eleven wine-producing countries. Under the care and guidance of Tony, Bill, and John Terlato, an additional 60 acres were planted to Cabernet Sauvignon, and a new state-of-the-art winery facility was built. After Hack Wilson's death, the Terlato family assumed full ownership of the winery, a gem that includes 119 acres of vineyard devoted almost entirely to the winery's signature: Cabernet Sauvignon and other Bordeaux varietals. Over the past decade, the Terlato family has carried the winery and its legacy forward by continuing to produce handcrafted, small-production, single-vineyard wines.

From behind the stately wine bar, staffers warmly greet guests. Just outside the tasting room, a patio with tables and lounge furniture arranged under a wisteria-draped arbor makes a perfect setting to relax with a glass of wine. From this vantage point, visitors can admire Ganymede, the gardens, and, beyond the old winery, the Stags Leap Palisades. To the east is the V-shaped formation where an indigenous Wappo hunter once reported seeing a legendary stag make a diversionary leap to save its herd from flying arrows.

CLOS DU VAL

That this winery has a French name is not an affectation. Owner and cofounder John Goelet's mother was a direct descendant of Françoise Guestier, a native of Bordeaux who worked for the Marquis de Segur, owner of Chateau Lafite and Latour. Clos Du Val translates as "small vineyard estate of a small valley," a modest nomenclature for a winery of its stature.

When Goelet, who is also the son of an American entrepreneur, set out on a global search for premium vineyard land, he found the ideal partner in Bernard Portet. Born in Cognac and raised in Bordeaux, Portet is a descendant of six generations of winemakers. He followed his passion with formal studies at the French winemaking schools of Toulouse and Montpelier before Goelet hired him in 1970 to establish Clos Du Val.

Portet spent two years searching six continents before getting a taste of the Napa Valley climate — or, technically, its microclimates. At the time, the cool evenings and dramatic terrain of the Stags Leap District were relatively undiscovered by winemakers. Goelet proved his faith in Portet by promptly acquiring 150 acres of land in the district. The first vintage of the new venture was a 1972 Cabernet Sauvignon, one of only six California Cabernets selected for the now-legendary Paris tasting in 1976, an event that put the world on notice that Napa Valley was a winemaking force to watch. Ten years later, the same vintage took first place in a rematch, further enhancing Clos Du Val's reputation for creating wines that stand the test of time.

In 1973 Clos Du Val purchased 180 acres in another little-recognized appellation — Carneros in southern Napa. Thirteen years later, the winery released its first Carneros Chardonnay, and four years later, its first Carneros Pinot Noir.

A driveway lined with cypress trees leads to the imposing, vine-covered stone winery, behind which the dramatic rock outcroppings of Stags Leap rise in sharp relief. In front of the tasting room are Mediterranean-style gardens, a raised lawn area with tables and chairs defined by a hedge of boxwood, and a demonstration vineyard with twenty rows of Merlot grapevines, accompanied by brief explanations of vineyard management techniques. Inside the winery, halogen lights on the high ceiling beam down on the wooden tasting bar, the unglazed earth-toned tile floor, and a corner display of merchandise bearing the winery's distinctive, curlicued logo. Glass doors on the far side look into a large fermentation room filled with oak and steel tanks. Visitors are welcome to prolong their visit by playing *pétanque* or enjoying a picnic in the olive grove.

CLOS DU VAL
5330 Silverado Trail
Napa, CA 94558
707-261-5200
800-993-9463
cdv@closduval.com
www.closduval.com

OWNER: John Goelet.

LOCATION: 5 miles north of the town of Napa.

APPELLATION: Stags Leap District.

HOURS: 10 A.M.–5 P.M. daily.

TASTINGS: $15 for current releases; $25 for reserve tasting.

TOURS: By appointment.

THE WINES: Cabernet Sauvignon, Chardonnay, Merlot, Pinot Noir.

SPECIALTY: Cabernet Sauvignon.

WINEMAKERS: John Clews and Kristy Melton.

ANNUAL PRODUCTION: 60,000 cases.

OF SPECIAL NOTE: Cabanas for outdoor tastings. Private tastings and cheese pairings by appointment. *Pétanque* court and picnic areas. Demonstration vineyard for self-guided walks. Winery and picnic grounds are pet friendly.

NEARBY ATTRACTIONS: Napa Valley Opera House (live performances in historic building); Napa Valley Museum (winemaking displays, art exhibits).

CUVAISON ESTATE WINES

CUVAISON ESTATE WINES
CARNEROS TASTING ROOM:
1221 Duhig Rd.
Napa, CA 94559
707-942-2455
appointments@cuvaison.
com
www.cuvaison.com

CALISTOGA TASTING ROOM:
4550 Silverado Trail
Calistoga, CA 94515
707-942-2468
tastingroom@cuvaison.com

OWNER:
Thomas Schmidheiny.

LOCATIONS: Carneros:
2 miles west of Hwy. 12.
Calistoga: 3 miles east of
downtown Calistoga.

APPELLATIONS: Los
Carneros, Mount Veeder.

HOURS: 10 A.M.–5 P.M. daily
(both locations).

TASTINGS: Calistoga:
$15–$20. Group cave
tastings, $25 per person,
6-person minimum, by
appointment. Carneros:
$20, by appointment.

TOURS: Carneros vineyard
walk and tasting ($30),
Friday–Monday, 9:30 A.M.,
by appointment.

THE WINES: Cabernet Sauvignon, Chardonnay, Es-
piritu (dessert-style wine),
Pinot Noir, Sauvignon
Blanc, Syrah, Zinfandel.

SPECIALTIES: Cabernet
Sauvignon, Chardonnay,
Pinot Noir, Syrah.

WINEMAKER: Steven Rogstad.

ANNUAL PRODUCTION:
55,000 cases.

OF SPECIAL NOTE: With
advance order, Calistoga
location will provide picnic
lunch.

NEARBY ATTRACTIONS:
Carneros: di Rosa Preserve
(indoor and outdoor exhibits
of works by contemporary
Bay Area artists). Calistoga:
Robert Louis Stevenson
State Park (hiking).

Visitors to Cuvaison Estate Wines in Carneros venture into the very heart of the winery's estate vineyard. Originally planted in 1980, the vineyard offers a brush with local history, for it was among the first in Carneros dedicated to Chardonnay and Pinot Noir. Four hundred acres of vines surround the elegant tasting room, which stands atop a gentle slope. The structure features clean lines and walls of reclaimed redwood set against the glint of an aluminum awning at the entryway. Built in 2009, it is the newer of the winery's two different tasting rooms.

Inside, floor-to-ceiling sliding glass doors frame seemingly endless vineyard views. A reservoir sparkles in the near distance, and oak-dotted Milliken Peak rises against the sky. Visitors enjoy seated tastings of the entirely estate-grown wines—primarily Chardonnay, Pinot Noir, and Cabernet Sauvignon—at tall bistro tables with matching chairs made of recycled aluminum. Hanging white globe lamps offer gentle illumination, and a zinc counter glows above slate flooring.

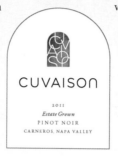

In warm weather, staffers open the glass doors to admit breezes from nearby San Pablo Bay and link the room with an outdoor deck, where teak tables and chairs accommo- date seated tastings or leisurely scenery gazing. The tasting room anchors a complex that includes a 20,000-square-foot, solar-powered winery and a smaller barrel room.

Founded in 1969, Cuvaison was Napa Valley's twenty-seventh official winery. The name was taken from a French word that describes the mingling of grape juice with seeds and skins to allow extraction of color and flavor. In 1979 the winery was purchased by the Schmidheinys, a Swiss family whose holdings include a vineyard in Switzerland. That same year, the family bought the Carneros vineyard site, where they planted Burgundian varieties and would eventually build their production facility. In 1998 the family acquired the historic Brandlin Vineyard on Mount Veeder to augment their Bordeaux-style wine program.

Cuvaison's original tasting room is thirty miles north, near Calistoga, amid the oak and pine forests of Napa Valley's northeastern foothills. Tunneled into the mountain behind the tasting room are caves providing 22,000 square feet of climate-controlled barrel storage. The amiable servers offer both bar-side and seated tastings. Visitors who have packed a picnic lunch are encouraged to relax at tables on the shaded lawn or beside the olive grove.

DOMAINE CARNEROS

An architectural tribute to its French heritage, the impressive Domaine Carneros château would look at home in Champagne, France. Crowning a hillside in the Carneros region of southern Napa, it is situated in a prime growing area for Chardonnay and Pinot Noir, the primary grape varieties used in sparkling wine. A grand staircase framed by fountains and gardens forms the entrance to the winery. French marble floors, high ceilings, and decorative features such as a Louis XV fireplace mantel impart a palatial ambience. Guests savor wines and food pairings seated at their choice of a private table in the elegant salon, warmed by a fireplace on cool days, or on the broad, sunny terrace with its panoramic views of the surrounding vineyards.

Domaine Carneros started with a quest by Claude Taittinger of Champagne Taittinger in Reims, France, for an ideal site in California for growing and producing world-class sparkling wine. He found it in the Carneros, where a long, moderately cool growing season and breezes from San Pablo Bay allow for slow, even ripening, mature flavors, and bright acidity in Pinot Noir and Chardonnay grapes. Established in 1987, Domaine Carneros now includes four certified organic estate vineyards for a total of 350 acres.

Harvest at Domaine Carneros typically begins in mid-August, when the delicate balance between sugar and acidity is at the optimal point for sparkling wines. Crews head out to pick grapes before dawn, and the fruit is immediately brought to the winery for gentle pressing. Each lot is maintained separately until the perfect blend is determined. At Domaine Carneros, sparkling wines are made in accordance with the rigorous and complex *méthode champenoise*, in which secondary fermentation takes place in the bottle. A growing portfolio of fine Pinot Noir still wines has aficionados of the Burgundian varietal praising the winery's production and the expertise of Pinot Noir winemaker TJ Evans.

Heading this multifaceted operation is founding winemaker/CEO Eileen Crane, who has been with Domaine Carneros from the beginning—helping to locate the winery site and develop the vineyards and facilities. In addition to serving as one of California's pioneering women in wine, Crane has led the way in sustainable grape growing and winemaking. Domaine Carneros became the first sparkling winery in the United States to receive organic certification for 100 percent of its estate vineyards.

DOMAINE CARNEROS

1240 Duhig Rd.
Napa, CA 94559
800-716-BRUT (2788)
707-257-0101
www.domainecarneros.
com

OWNERS: Partnership between Taittinger and Kopf families.

LOCATION: Intersection of Hwys. 121/12 and Duhig Rd., 4 miles southwest of the town of Napa and 6 miles southeast of Sonoma.

APPELLATION: Los Carneros.

HOURS: 10 A.M.–6 P.M. daily.

TASTINGS: Seated tastings; reservations recommended. $20–$30 (varies by tasting selected). Groups of 10 or more by appointment.

TOURS: 11 A.M., 1 P.M., and 3 P.M. daily. Additional tours offered seasonally. Group tours for 10 or more by appointment.

THE WINES: Brut Rosé, Le Rêve, Pinot Noir, Vintage Brut.

SPECIALTIES: *Méthode champenoise* sparkling wine, Pinot Noir.

WINEMAKERS: Eileen Crane, founding winemaker; TJ Evans, Pinot Noir winemaker.

ANNUAL PRODUCTION: 48,000 cases.

OF SPECIAL NOTE: Table service in salon or on terrace with panoramic views of Carneros region. Cheese and caviar available for purchase.

NEARBY ATTRACTIONS: di Rosa Preserve (indoor and outdoor exhibits of works by contemporary Bay Area artists); Napa Valley Opera House.

EHLERS ESTATE

EHLERS ESTATE
3222 Ehlers Ln.
St. Helena, CA 94574
707-963-5972
info@ehlersestate.com
www.ehlersestate.com

OWNER: Leducq Foundation.

LOCATION: 3 miles north of St. Helena.

APPELLATION: St. Helena.

HOURS: 10:30 A.M.–4 P.M. daily.

TASTINGS: By appointment only ($25–$50).

TOURS: Offered with chocolate-and-wine pairing.

THE WINES: Cabernet Franc, Cabernet Sauvignon "1886," J. Leducq Cabernet Sauvignon, Merlot, Sauvignon Blanc.

SPECIALTY: Cabernet Sauvignon "1886".

WINEMAKER: Kevin Morrisey.

ANNUAL PRODUCTION: 8,000 cases.

OF SPECIAL NOTE: Cabernet Franc, J. Leducq, and Petit Verdot available only in the tasting room.

NEARBY ATTRACTIONS: Culinary Institute of America at Greystone (cooking demonstrations); Bothe-Napa State Park (hiking, picnicking, horseback riding, swimming Memorial Day–Labor Day); Bale Grist Mill State Historic Park (water-powered mill circa 1846); Silverado Museum (Robert Louis Stevenson memorabilia).

In St. Helena, at the narrowest part of Napa Valley, just off Highway 29, Ehlers Estate offers a glimpse into the rural heart of wine country. At the entrance, an antique grape press atop a stone base towers eight feet beside olive trees planted more than a century ago. Beyond lie a demonstration vineyard, a raised-bed vegetable garden, and a sculpture of brightly painted grapevines. Low rock walls, oaks, and the winery itself sit at the center of one of Napa Valley's rare, contiguous estate vineyards. Consisting primarily of Cabernet Sauvignon, the vineyard is certified organic and biodynamic, and all the fruit is estate grown, giving the winemaker full control from vine to bottle.

Ehlers Estate boasts both a modern winemaking facility and a nineteenth-century winery, built in 1886 of tuff and basalt and currently serving as the tasting room. Etched above the arched doorway, builder Bernard Ehlers's name can still be seen. A Sacramento grocer, Ehlers bought the property from a viticulturist who had lost his vines to phylloxera. He replanted the vineyard, and after his death in 1901, the winery operated under a variety of different names. In 1987 French entrepreneur and philanthropist Jean Leducq and his wife, Sylviane, purchased seven acres of Ehlers's original holdings. By 2001, they acquired thirty-five more acres to create the estate and restored the Ehlers name to the property.

Jean Leducq was born in 1919 and grew up in Paris. Even as a small child, he was influenced by his family's passion for food and wine. In 1968 he took over his grandfather's linen service. Thirty years later, having expanded into parts of Europe and the United States, the business ranked as the largest family-owned company in France. When he sold the company, Leducq and his wife created the Leducq Foundation to fund international cardiovascular research. As an asset of the trust, Ehlers Estate returns 100 percent of the winery profits to this prestigious foundation.

Under the guidance of winemaker Kevin Morrisey, Ehlers Estate makes small-production, handcrafted Bordeaux varietals. Morrisey, former winemaker at Napa Valley's historic Stags' Leap Winery, holds a master's degree from UC Davis and interned at Pomerol's legendary Château Pétrus. He spent nearly ten years at Stags' Leap, where he confirmed his reputation for making complex, *terroir*-driven wine.

Inside the historic stone winery, guests enjoy a hospitable and inviting sit-down tasting. The winery also offers a "perfectly paired" wine and chocolate experience, which includes a barrel tasting and a stroll around the property and features custom, handcrafted chocolates designed to perfectly showcase the estate-grown red wines.

ETUDE WINES

Napa Valley is renowned for its rugged foothills and sun-drenched vineyards, but in its southwestern reaches, visitors find lush, naturally occurring wetlands. Part of the Carneros appellation, this secluded corner supports scores of birds, as well as mature stands of oaks and California bay trees. Here, the marine influence from nearby San Pablo Bay moderates summer heat, helping to extend the growing season for Pinot Noir, Etude's signature wine.

Unlike the sedimentary clay under most Carneros vineyards, the soils of Etude's 1,300-acre property are rocky, well drained, and volcanic, making them ideal for growing Burgundian varieties. Planted to conform  to the changing topography, Etude's vineyard rows run at diverse angles, and blocks average only eight acres. Close spacing of the vines produces low yields of highly flavorful fruit. With four protected wetlands on the property, winery workers take extra care to farm sustainably and keep waterways clean. In fact, having met rigorous standards set by state and federal water quality laws, Etude has received Napa Green and Fish Friendly Farming certification.

Etude Wines was founded in 1980 by winemaker Tony Soter, who believed that improved vineyard practices reduced the need for vinicultural intervention. The winery embraces the philosophy that winemaking begins in the vineyard, and the result is a portfolio of distinguished wines, each expressing authentic varietal characteristics. Etude released its first Napa Valley Cabernet Sauvignon in 1980 and continues to source fruit from prime Cabernet Sauvignon benchlands located throughout Napa Valley, including those in the Rutherford, Oakville, St. Helena, and Calistoga appellations. With the release of its first Carneros Pinot Noir in 1982, the winery launched its acclaimed Pinot Noir program, which features a seven-acre estate vineyard dedicated to rare clones of the grape.

In 2005 winemaker Jon Priest moved from the Central Coast to practice his craft alongside Soter. Priest had worked for more than a dozen years at Wild Horse Winery, where he made upward of thirty varietals, before moving to Adelaida Cellars, and then to TAZ Vineyards, in 2003. He harbors a special fondness for Pinot Noir, savoring the challenges posed by the finicky grape, as well as the pure pleasure it delivers when handled correctly.

In 2009 Etude Wines opened a new tasting room, an elegant space with blond oak paneling and an intricately patterned floor made from end-cut Douglas fir. Embedded rice hulls add a pleasant texture to the concrete tasting bar, and on the wall behind it, a backlit rack holds rows of wine bottles that glow like colorful works of art.

ETUDE WINES
1250 Cuttings Wharf Rd.
Napa, CA 94558
877-586-9361
www.etudewines.com

OWNER: Treasury Wine Estates.

LOCATION: About 4 miles southwest of the city of Napa.

APPELLATION: Los Carneros.

HOURS: 10 A.M.–4:30 P.M. daily.

TASTINGS: $15 for 5 wines; $25 for 5 reserve wines. $35 for 6 wines paired with 3 savory bites, 10 A.M., 1 P.M., and 3 P.M., Friday–Sunday, by appointment.

TOURS: None.

THE WINES: Cabernet Sauvignon, Chardonnay, Pinot Blanc, Pinot Gris, Pinot Noir, Rosé of Pinot Noir.

SPECIALTIES: Chardonnay, Napa Valley Cabernet, Estate Pinot Noir.

WINEMAKER: Jon Priest.

ANNUAL PRODUCTION: 28,000 cases.

OF SPECIAL NOTE: Picnic tables available with advance reservation. Winery is pet friendly. Rutherford, St. Helena, and Oakville Cabernet Sauvignon, Pinot Blanc, and Temblor Pinot Noir sold in tasting room only.

NEARBY ATTRACTIONS: di Rosa Preserve (indoor and outdoor exhibits of works by contemporary Bay Area artists); Napa Valley Opera House (live performances in historic building).

FRANK FAMILY VINEYARDS

FRANK FAMILY VINEYARDS
1091 Larkmead Ln.
Calistoga, CA 94515
800-574-9463
www.frankfamily
vineyards.com

OWNERS: Frank family.

LOCATION: About 5 miles north of St. Helena via Hwy. 29.

APPELLATION: Napa Valley.

HOURS: 10 A.M.–5 P.M. daily.

TASTINGS: $20; $30 for reserve tasting.

TOURS: None.

THE WINES: Cabernet Sauvignon, Champagne, Chardonnay, late-harvest Chardonnay, Pinot Noir, Port, Sangiovese, Zinfandel.

SPECIALTIES: Cabernet Sauvignon from Rutherford, Champagne, Chardonnay.

WINEMAKER: Todd Graff.

ANNUAL PRODUCTION: 50,000 cases.

OF SPECIAL NOTE: Reserve Lewis Chardonnay, Pinot Noir, Sangiovese, and Zinfandel; Rutherford Reserve Cabernet; Winston Hill Red Wine; and *méthode champenoise* wines available only at winery.

NEARBY ATTRACTIONS: Bothe-Napa State Park; Robert Louis Stevenson State Park; Old Faithful Geyser of California; Petrified Forest; Sharpsteen Museum (exhibits on Robert Louis Stevenson and Walt Disney animator Ben Sharpsteen).

At a time when many Napa Valley wineries are increasingly exclusive, the convivial, unpretentious ambience at Frank Family Vineyards is decidedly refreshing. Yet this is not the only reason for heading slightly off the beaten path to reach this historic property. Frank Family Vineyards is home to a massive stone building constructed in 1884 as Larkmead Winery, the third oldest winery in Napa. Refurbished in 1906 with sandstone from the nearby hills, the structure is listed on the National Register of Historic Places and as an official Point of Historical Interest in the state of California.

In 1992 Rich and Connie Frank had the opportunity to purchase the Kornell Champagne Cellars at Larkmead Winery. Today, they continue to produce Champagne in the old cellar, where thick stone walls, high-stacked barrels, and the unmistakable bouquet of aging wines impart an almost palpable sense of history. Winemaker Todd Graff handcrafts Blanc de Blancs, Blanc de Noirs, Rouge, and Reserve in the traditional French *méthode champenoise* style. Visitors can see the equipment Graff uses to produce 2,200 cases of Champagne each year.

The focus at Frank Family Vineyards, however, is largely on still wines, using grapes from three distinguished Napa vineyards. Winston Hill, Rich Frank's personal estate, rises five hundred feet above the valley floor in Rutherford and produces Cabernet Sauvignon, as well as small amounts of Merlot, Cabernet Franc, and Sangiovese. The grapes from this vineyard are used for Frank Family's estate wines—Winston Hill Red Wine, Rutherford Reserve Cabernet, and Rutherford Reserve Sangiovese. Fruit for the winery's Napa Valley Cabernet Sauvignon comes from the S&J Vineyard in the Capell Valley, located east of the Vaca Range. Frank Family's Lewis Vineyard at Buchli Station is in the heart of Carneros, where the combination of cool maritime climate and shallow, dense clay loam soils produces lively, well-balanced Chardonnay and Pinot Noir. Frank Family also makes a Zinfandel Port and a late-harvest Chardonnay, both available in very small quantities at the winery.

As former president of Disney Studios, Rich Frank knows how to make visitors feel welcome. The tasting room, at times brimming with laughter, has been recognized among the top in the country, and the winery, consistently among the best in Napa in Bay Area polls. Located in a remodeled Craftsman house, the tasting room provides separate areas for sampling Champagne and still wines. Outside, visitors are welcome to relax at wooden picnic tables under statuesque elm trees and enjoy the spectacular vineyard views.

GRGICH HILLS ESTATE

Few people driving along Highway 29 recognize both of the red, white, and blue flags flying in front of this winery. They certainly know one, the American flag. The other represents Croatia, the native country of winemaker and co-owner Miljenko "Mike" Grgich.

The simple red-tile-roofed, white stucco building may not be as flashy as those of nearby wineries, but as the saying goes, it's what's inside that counts. Once visitors pass beneath the grapevine trellis and into the dimly lit recesses of the tasting room, they forget about exterior appearances. The comfortable, old-world atmosphere at Grgich Hills Estate is not a gimmick.

The winery was founded "GUR-gitch") and Austin E. Hills well known. Hills is a member ily. Grgich was virtually legend-drawn worldwide attention in Paris tasting, an all-French panel Montelena Chardonnay over the  by Mike Grgich (pronounced on July 4, 1977. Both were already of the Hills Brothers coffee fam-ary, especially in France. He had 1976, when, at the now-famous of judges chose his 1973 Chateau best of the white Burgundies in a blind tasting. It was a momentous occasion for the California wine industry in general and in particular for Mike Grgich, who was already acknowledged as one of the state's top winemakers.

Finally in a position to capitalize on his fame, Grgich quickly found a simpatico partner in Hills, who had a background in business and finance and was the owner of established vineyards. The two men shortly began turning out the intensely flavored Chardonnays that remain the flagship wines of Grgich Hills Estate.

Grgich, easily recognizable with his trademark blue beret, was born in 1923 into a winemaking family on the Dalmatian coast of Croatia. He arrived in California in 1958 and spent his early years at Beaulieu Vineyard, where he worked with the late, pioneering winemaker André Tchelistcheff before moving on to Mondavi and Chateau Montelena. Grgich continues to make wine and relies on a younger generation—daughter Violet Grgich, vice president of sales and marketing, and nephew Ivo Jeramaz, vice president of production and vineyard development—to carry on the family tradition. Visitors may well run into family members when taking the exceptionally informative winery tour or while sampling wines in the cool, cellarlike tasting room or in the VIP tasting room and hospitality center.

GRGICH HILLS ESTATE
1829 St. Helena Hwy.
Rutherford, CA 94573
800-532-3057
info@grgich.com
www.grgich.com

OWNERS: Miljenko "Mike" Grgich and Austin Hills.

LOCATION: About 3 miles south of St. Helena.

APPELLATION: Napa Valley.

HOURS: 9:30 A.M.–4:30 P.M. daily.

TASTINGS: $20 for 5 wines.

TOURS: By appointment, 11 A.M. and 2 P.M. daily.

THE WINES: Cabernet Sauvignon, Chardonnay, Fumé Blanc, Merlot, Violetta (late-harvest dessert wine), Zinfandel.

SPECIALTY: Chardonnay.

WINEMAKER: Mike Grgich.

ANNUAL PRODUCTION: 65,000 cases.

OF SPECIAL NOTE: Barrel tastings held 2–4 P.M. on Friday afternoons, except during harvest, when grape stomping is offered daily. Napa Valley Wine Train stops at Grgich Hills for special tour and tasting; call 800-427-4124 for schedule.

NEARBY ATTRACTIONS: Bothe-Napa State Park (hiking, picnicking, horseback riding, swimming Memorial Day–Labor Day); Bale Grist Mill State Historic Park (water-powered mill circa 1846); Silverado Museum (Robert Louis Stevenson memorabilia).

HEITZ WINE CELLARS

HEITZ WINE CELLARS
Tasting and Sales Room:
436 St. Helena Hwy. South
St. Helena, CA 94574
707-963-3542
Mailing Address:
500 Taplin Rd.
St. Helena, CA 94574
www.heitzcellar.com

OWNERS: Heitz family.

LOCATION: 2 miles south of St. Helena.

APPELLATION: Napa Valley.

HOURS: 11 A.M.–4:30 P.M. daily.

TASTINGS: Complimentary.

TOURS: Of winery by appointment.

THE WINES: Cabernet Sauvignon, Chardonnay, Grignolino, Port, Sauvignon Blanc, Zinfandel.

SPECIALTY: Vineyard-designated Cabernet Sauvignon.

WINEMAKER: David Heitz.

ANNUAL PRODUCTION: 40,000 cases.

OF SPECIAL NOTE: The only Napa Valley producer of Grignolino, a red Italian wine grape commonly grown in the Piedmont region.

NEARBY ATTRACTIONS: Culinary Institute of America at Greystone (cooking demonstrations); Bothe-Napa State Park (hiking, picnicking, horseback riding, swimming Memorial Day–Labor Day); Bale Grist Mill State Historic Park (water-powered mill circa 1846); Silverado Museum (Robert Louis Stevenson memorabilia).

In 1961, when Joe and Alice Heitz produced their first bottle of wine, they never dreamed that one day Heitz wines would grace dining tables across the country and even around the world. The couple started Heitz Wine Cellars on an eight-acre vineyard just south of St. Helena when Napa Valley had fewer than twenty wineries. As news spread about the quality of the wines, their business grew. In 1964 the Heitzes acquired 160 acres of pristine farmland in the gently sloping hills near the Silverado Trail. This property, which included an historic stone cellar built in 1898, became the heart of their family business.

Two of their earliest visitors were Tom and Martha May, owners of Martha's Vineyard in Oakville. The Heitzes agreed to purchase their fruit, and when Joe Heitz crafted an especially remarkable Cabernet Sauvignon from the 1966 vintage, the two families decided to put the vineyard's name on the bottle, creating the first Napa Valley Cabernet with vineyard designation. Martha's Vineyard Cabernet Sauvignon is now one of the most widely recognized wines in the world, and the Heitz family's exclusive arrangement to produce wine from the Martha's Vineyard grapes continues today. Heitz Trailside Vineyard and Napa Valley Cabernets have also earned acclaim.

Joe Heitz was a founder of the "new" winery movement that focused on boutique wines. At the time, long-established big wineries still planted vines that produced the highest yields, rather than nurturing the best grapes for each location. Offering fresh insights and taking bold steps earned Heitz the admiration of generations of California winemakers, as well as induction in 2012 into the Hall of Fame at the Culinary Institute of America.

The second generation now leads the family business. President Kathleen Heitz Myers and winemaker David Heitz have made their mark by skillfully balancing innovative business practices and signature winemaking traditions. Myers carries on the family legacy of leadership in the wine industry by serving as 2012–2013 chair of the California Wine Institute board of directors and, in 2011–2012, as president of the Napa Valley Vintners. In 2002, at the site of the original winery, the family built a new sales and tasting room of native stone. On a back patio, visitors can admire panoramic views within feet of the first Cabernet Sauvignon vines. The majority of the Heitz vineyards, including this one, are certified organic. As the Heitzes celebrate the milestone of their fifty-second anniversary, a third generation has joined the business. Heitz Wine Cellars is one of the few wineries established during the renaissance of Napa Valley winemaking to remain family owned.

THE HESS COLLECTION WINERY

A gently winding road heads up a forested mountainside to this winery on the western rim of the Napa Valley. Although only a fifteen-minute drive from bustling Highway 29, the estate feels a thousand times removed. Arriving visitors are greeted with stunning vineyard views from almost every vantage point.

Swiss entrepreneur Donald Hess has owned vineyards on Mount Veeder since 1978, so when he decided to establish his own winery, he didn't have to look far to find the Christian Brothers Mont La Salle property. He already knew that the east side of the extinct volcano provides a cool climate that allows a long growing season as well as excellent soil drainage—two viticultural components known for producing Cabernet Sauvignon with excellent structure and superb concentration of aromas and flavors. Vineyards were first planted on this land in the 1860s, long before the ivy-clad, three-story stone winery was built in 1903. The Christian Brothers produced wine here for nearly a half century before leasing the facilities to Hess in 1986. He began planting Cabernet Sauvignon vineyards on terrain so steep they have to be picked by hand. The vines must grow extended roots to cling to the mountainside, and the resultant stress creates fruit of exceptional character.

The Hess Collection farms 310 acres of Mount Veeder vineyards that range in elevation from six hundred to two thousand feet. Viewing itself as a steward of the land, the winery farms these vineyards using the principles of sustainable and organic agriculture. The vineyards and winery have been certified by the Napa Green program of the Napa Valley Vintners.

Hess spent three years renovating the facility before opening it to the public in 1989. The overhaul included transforming 13,000 square feet on the second and third floors to display his extensive collection of international art, which consists of 143 paintings, sculptures, and interactive pieces by modern and contemporary artists, among them such luminaries as Francis Bacon, Frank Stella, Anselm Kiefer, Andy Goldsworthy, and Robert Motherwell. One work evokes a particularly strong response for its social commentary. It is Argentinean Leopold Maler's *Hommage 1974*, an eternally burning typewriter created in protest of the repression of artistic freedom.

The tasting room, which shares the first floor with a century-old barrel-aging cellar, is built from a local metamorphic sandstone called rhyolite. The stone had been covered with stucco by the Christian Brothers but was inadvertently exposed during the winery's renovation. This is where visitors linger and share their impressions of both the wine and the art.

THE HESS COLLECTION WINERY
4411 Redwood Rd.
Napa, CA 94558
707-255-8584
www.hesscollection.com

FOUNDER: Donald Hess.

LOCATION: 7 miles west of Hwy. 29.

APPELLATIONS: Mount Veeder, Napa Valley.

HOURS: 10 A.M.–5:30 P.M. daily.

TASTINGS: $10–$25. Various food-and-wine pairings ($20–$75) at 10 A.M. and 2 P.M. on Thursday, Friday, and Saturday by reservation.

TOURS: Art collection open daily; museum admission is free. Guided tours of winery and collection available.

THE WINES: Cabernet Sauvignon, Chardonnay, 19 Block Cuvée, Petite Sirah, Sauvignon Blanc, Viognier, Zinfandel.

SPECIALTIES: Mount Veeder Cabernet Sauvignon, Chardonnay, 19 Block Cuvée.

WINEMAKERS: David Guffy (Hess), Randle Johnson (Artezin).

ANNUAL PRODUCTION: Unavailable.

OF SPECIAL NOTE: Extensive collection of international art. Many wines available only in tasting room.

NEARBY ATTRACTIONS: di Rosa Preserve (indoor and outdoor exhibits of works by contemporary artists); Alston Regional Park (hiking).

INGLENOOK

INGLENOOK
1991 St. Helena Hwy.
Rutherford, CA 94573
707-968-1161
800-782-4266
reservations@inglenook.
com
www.inglenook.com

OWNERS: Francis and
Eleanor Coppola.

LOCATION: About 3 miles
south of St. Helena.

APPELLATIONS: Rutherford,
Napa Valley.

HOURS: Château: 11 A.M.–
5 P.M. daily. Bistro: 10 A.M.–
5 P.M. daily.

TASTINGS: $50 for sit-down
tasting of 4 estate wines.
Reservation required.

TOURS: 11 A.M., 1:30 P.M.,
and 3 P.M. daily.
Reservation required
(707-968-1161).

THE WINES: Blancaneaux
(white blend), CASK
Cabernet Sauvignon,
Edizione Pennino
Zinfandel, RC Reserve
Syrah, Rubicon (flagship
red blend).

SPECIALTY: Rubicon.

WINEMAKER:
Philippe Bascaules.

ANNUAL PRODUCTION:
Unavailable.

OF SPECIAL NOTE: Extensive
shop with estate olive oil,
books, wine accessories,
and gifts. More than
200 acres of organically
certified vineyards. Wines
by the glass, espresso, sodas,
and light snacks offered at
the Bistro Wine Bar.

NEARBY ATTRACTIONS:
Silverado Museum
(Robert Louis Stevenson
memorabilia); Napa Valley
Museum (winemaking
displays, art exhibits);
Culinary Institute of
America at Greystone
(cooking demonstrations).

Inglenook was founded in 1879 by Finnish sea captain Gustave Niebaum, who made his fortune in the Alaska fur trade. He modeled the massive stone château after the estates he had visited in Bordeaux and imported the best European grapevines to plant nearby. By the time Francis and Eleanor Coppola entered the picture nearly a century later, however, a series of corporate ownerships had divided the estate and damaged its brand.

Seeking a weekend home in wine country, the Coppolas were shown the historic Niebaum mansion in 1975, the start of their thirty-five-year journey to restore the original estate and its label. By 1995, the Coppolas had acquired the major parcels of the original estate and renamed it Niebaum-Coppola. They replanted vineyards with the same type of rootstock originally used by the founder in the 1800s and began bringing the château and its grounds back to their former glory. The European-style front courtyard now features a redwood and stone pergola graced with grapevines and a ninety-by-thirty-foot reflecting pool that is illuminated at night. In the vaulted entrance is another of Francis Coppola's most dramatic creations: a grand staircase built of exotic hardwoods imported from Belize. The château also includes an exhibit celebrating milestones in Inglenook's long, illustrious history, including the production of the 1941 Cabernet Sauvignon, heralded as one of the greatest wines ever made.

When Coppola set out to craft a proprietary red wine using the acclaimed estate vineyards in 1978, he decided to call it Rubicon, signifying the point of no return. The Bordeaux-style blend remains the winery's flagship red wine. In 2011 Coppola acquired the iconic Inglenook trademark, restoring the estate's original name. At the same time, he brought on board Philippe Bascaules, former estate manager of Châteaux Margaux in Bordeaux, France.

Visitors may take part in one of three daily experiences, a ninety-minute tour, and a seated tasting with food accompaniments. Those seeking specialty experiences may opt for the Vinifera Journey, a vineyard stroll capped with a tasting of the flagship wine; the Sensory Exploration, a château tour followed by an exploration of flavors and aromas; the Elevage Experience, a detailed look at winemaking that ends with barrel samples and cheese in the caves; or the seasonally offered Janus, complete with a tour and seated, bountiful food-and-wine pairing in a private cellar. Inglenook also offers personalized private tours and tastings.

MARKHAM VINEYARDS

Few people are surprised to hear that Charles Krug, Schramsberg, and Sutter Home wineries were in business in 1874. Less widely known is that they were the only three wineries operating in Napa Valley that year, when Jean Laurent founded the St. Helena winery that, less than a century later, would become known as Markham Vineyards.

Laurent, a Frenchman from Bordeaux, arrived in California in 1852, drawn by the lure of the 1849 Gold Rush. When his prospecting failed to pan out, he made his way to the city of Napa in 1868 and began growing vegetables. Laurent quickly assessed the high quality of the soil and, being from Bordeaux, realized Napa Valley was ideally suited to grapevines. Six years later, he established the Laurent Winery in St. Helena. After Laurent died in 1890, the property changed hands a number of times. In 1977 it was purchased by Bruce Markham, who had already acquired prime vineyard land on the Napa Valley floor, including 93 acres in Yountville once owned by Inglenook. By 1978 he had added the Calistoga Ranch at the headlands of the Napa River and the Oak Knoll Vineyard in the Oak Knoll District. The Markham estate vineyards now cover a total of 330 acres, including the most recent acquisition, Trubody Vineyards, west of Yountville in the center of the valley. These four areas have distinct microclimates that contribute to the complexity of the various wines produced by the winery.

In 1988 the winery and vineyard holdings were sold to Japan's oldest and largest wine company, Mercian Corporation. Despite these changes, many things have remained constant. The current owners have maintained the winery's dedication to producing ultrapremium wines sold at relatively modest prices. The first employee hired by Markham, Bryan Del Bondio, a native of Napa Valley from a family immersed in winemaking, is now president of Markham Vineyards. Jean Laurent's original stone cellar sits at the heart of the facility.

Stylistically, the winery combines both historic and modern elements, with its old stone and concrete facade, and its subdued red metal roofing supported by round wooden columns. Koi ponds flank the approach to the tasting room, and beyond them, orange and yellow canna lilies provide bursts of color when the plants bloom in spring and summer. The tasting room has a large fireplace to warm visitors on cold days and an outdoor terrace to enjoy on sunny days. The Markham Gallery features artwork and photography by noted artists.

MARKHAM VINEYARDS
2812 St. Helena Hwy. North
St. Helena, CA 94574
707-963-5292
www.markhamvineyards.
com

OWNER:
Mercian Corporation.

LOCATION: 1 mile north of St. Helena on Hwy. 29.

APPELLATION: Napa Valley.

HOURS: 11 A.M.–5 P.M. daily.

TASTINGS: $15–$25 for current releases and library and estate selections.

TOURS: By appointment.

THE WINES: Cabernet Sauvignon, Chardonnay, Merlot, Sauvignon Blanc.

SPECIALTY: Merlot.

WINEMAKER:
Kimberlee Jackson Nicholls.

ANNUAL PRODUCTION:
100,000 cases.

OF SPECIAL NOTE: Visitor center, home of the Markham Gallery, hosts ongoing exhibits. Dinners in the historic stone cellar by appointment.

NEARBY ATTRACTIONS:
Bothe-Napa State Park (hiking, picnicking, horseback riding, swimming Memorial Day–Labor Day); Bale Grist Mill State Historic Park (water-powered mill circa 1846); Culinary Institute of America at Greystone (cooking demonstrations); Silverado Museum (Robert Louis Stevenson memorabilia).

Mumm Napa

Mumm Napa
8445 Silverado Trail
Rutherford, CA 94573
707-967-7700
mumm_info@
mummnapa.com
www.mummnapa.com

Owner: Pernod Ricard USA.

Location: East of
Rutherford, 1 mile south
of Rutherford Cross Rd.

Appellation: Napa Valley.

Hours: 10 A.M.–5 P.M. daily
(last seating at 4:45 P.M.).

Tastings: $10 and up for
flights, or by the flute.

Tours: 10 A.M., 11 A.M.,
1 P.M., and 3 P.M. daily.

The Wines: Blanc de Blancs,
Brut Prestige, Brut Rosé,
Demi Sec, DVX, Sparkling
Pinot Noir, Vintage Reserve.

Specialty: Sparkling wine
made in traditional French
style.

Winemaker:
Ludovic Dervin.

Annual Production:
250,000 cases.

Of Special Note: Permanent
collection of Ansel Adams
photography; exhibits of
internationally known
and local artists. Majority
of wines available only at
winery. Limited availability
of large-format bottles at
winery.

Nearby Attraction:
Napa Valley Museum
(winemaking displays,
art exhibits).

For connoisseurs of Champagne, relaxing outdoors on a sunny day with a glass of bubbly, in the company of good friends, with a panoramic vineyard view may be the ultimate pleasure. This is obviously what the founders of Mumm Napa had in mind when they conceived of establishing a winery in North America that could produce a sparkling wine that would live up to Champagne standards.

In 1979 representatives of Champagne Mumm of France began quietly searching for the ideal location for a winery. So secretive was their project that they even had a code name for it: Project Lafayette. The point man was  the late Guy Devaux, a native of Epernay, the epicenter of France's Champagne district and an expert on *méthode* *champenoise*. In this French style of winemaking, the wine undergoes its bubble-producing fermentation in the very bottle from which it will be drunk. Devaux criss- crossed the United States for four years before settling on Napa Valley, the country's best-known appellation.

The best way to appreciate Mumm Napa is to start with a tour. The winery has a reputation for putting on one of the best in the business, covering the complicated steps necessary to get all those bubbles into each bottle. The hour-long tour heads first to the demonstration garden, then proceeds to the winery. The best time of year to take the tour is during the harvest season, usually between mid-August and mid-October. However, there is a lot to see at any time of year.

Visitors enter the winery through the wine shop. Just beyond is the Oak Terrace, where guests can sample library wines, pair wines with artisan cheeses, and enjoy the spectacular views of the vineyards and the Mayacamas Range.

Mumm Napa is also noted for its fine art gallery. The winery exhibits the work of many renowned, as well as local, photographers in its expansive gallery. Guests may explore the gallery at their leisure, even while they enjoy a glass of sparkling wine.

Patz & Hall

The last place most people would think to look for a well-respected winery's tasting room would be in an anonymous complex of cookie-cutter office buildings. Granted, the exteriors are painted in a sophisticated palette of taupe and mauve. Only when the company's distinguished black and silver logo is close enough to see can visitors feel confident that they have arrived at the Patz & Hall Tasting Salon. The actual winemaking is done elsewhere, miles away on the east side of the town of Sonoma, where Patz & Hall established its own 30,000-square-foot winery in 2007 amid a fast-emerging neighborhood of similar facilities. Prior to that, Patz & Hall wines were produced at other Napa Valley wineries.

Patz & Hall was established in 1988, by four individuals—Donald Patz, James Hall, Anne Moses, and Heather Patz—who

dedicated themselves to making benchmark wines sourced from distinctive California vineyards. Today, they produce a total of fifteen Chardonnays and Pinot Noirs, all without owning a single vineyard themselves. The winery was founded on an unusual business model that began in the 1980s at Flora Springs Winery & Vineyards, when assistant winemaker James Hall and national sales manager Donald Patz forged a close friendship. Their mutual enthusiasm for wine produced from elite, small vineyards inspired them to blend their talents along with those of Anne Moses and Heather Patz. Together, the team boasted a wealth of knowledge and experience gleaned at such prestigious wineries as Far Niente, Girard Winery, and Honig Winery, where Hall was once the winemaker.

The founders apply their specialized expertise and daily attention to different areas of the family-run winery's operations. The cornerstone of Patz & Hall is this integrated, hands-on approach, combined with close personal relationships with growers who supply them with fruit from outstanding family-owned vineyards in Napa Valley, Russian River Valley, Mendocino County, Sonoma Coast, and Santa Lucia Highlands.

All along, the goal was to have a special place where they could welcome customers and get to know them in person. Opened in 2005 and freshly refurbished in 2008, the Patz & Hall Tasting Salon offers visitors two environments for wine and seasonal food pairings: the tasting bar that was added to the front room and a private salon beyond, where the bustle at most winery tasting rooms seems worlds away. In this secluded space, which is decorated like an exquisite dining room, guided tastings are held at a rectangular table made from reclaimed cherry wood and surrounded by eight chic straight-back chairs covered in a palomino shade of suede. Over the course of an hour or more, guests sample six wines paired with local farmstead cheeses and other light fare.

PATZ & HALL
851 Napa Valley Corporate Way, Suite A
Napa, CA 94558
877-265-6700
info@patzhall.com
www.patzhall.com

OWNERS: Donald Patz, Heather Patz, James Hall, and Anne Moses.

LOCATION: 4 miles south of downtown Napa.

APPELLATION: Napa Valley.

HOURS: 10 A.M.–4 P.M. Wednesday–Sunday.

TASTINGS: $40 for 6 wines paired with food complements by advance reservation. $20 for 4 wines at Salon Bar without reservation.

TOURS: None.

THE WINES: Chardonnay, Pinot Noir.

SPECIALTIES: Single-vineyard-designated wines.

WINEMAKER: James Hall.

ANNUAL PRODUCTION: 26,000 cases.

OF SPECIAL NOTE: Patz & Hall wines are available for sale at the tasting bar without advance reservations during regular operating hours.

NEARBY ATTRACTIONS: Napa Valley Wine Train (lunch, brunch, and dinner excursions); Napa Valley Opera House (theatrical and musical performances in historic building).

PEJU

PEJU
8466 St. Helena Hwy.
(Hwy. 29)
Rutherford, CA 94573
707-963-3600
800-446-7358
info@peju.com
www.peju.com

OWNERS: Anthony and
Herta Peju.

LOCATION: 11 miles north
of the town of Napa.

APPELLATIONS: Rutherford,
Napa Valley.

HOURS: 10 A.M.–6 P.M. daily.

TASTINGS: $20.

TOURS: Self-guided or by
appointment.

THE WINES: Cabernet Franc,
Cabernet Sauvignon,
Chardonnay, Merlot,
Provence, Sauvignon Blanc,
Syrah, Zinfandel.

SPECIALTIES: Reserve
Cabernet Sauvignon,
H.B. Vineyard Cabernet
Sauvignon, Fifty/fifty
(Bordeaux blend).

WINEMAKER: Sara Fowler.

ANNUAL PRODUCTION:
35,000 cases.

OF SPECIAL NOTE: Wine-
and-food pairings, cooking
classes, gift boutique. Barrel
tasting by reservation. Art
gallery featuring work by
contemporary artists. Many
wines available only at
winery.

NEARBY ATTRACTIONS:
Silverado Museum
(Robert Louis Stevenson
memorabilia); Napa Valley
Museum (winemaking
displays, art exhibits);
Culinary Institute of
America at Greystone
(cooking demonstrations).

Spotting Peju, even on a winery-lined stretch of Highway 29, is easy, thanks to a fifty-foot-tall tasting tower topped with a distinctive copper roof. Although the tasting tower opened only in late 2003, the structure looks as if it has been there for decades. Like the rest of the property, it could have been transplanted directly from the countryside of southern France.

The Rutherford estate had been producing wine grapes for more than eighty years when Anthony and Herta Peju bought it in 1982. The couple has been improving the thirty-acre property ever since, streamlining vineyard techniques and adding Merlot and Cabernet Franc grapes to the estate's core product, Cabernet Sauvignon. By the mid-1990s, demand for Peju wines outstripped the winery's supply. To satisfy it, the Pejus acquired a 350-acre property in northern Napa County in Pope Valley, planted a variety of grapes, and named it Persephone Vineyard, after a goddess in Greek mythology.

Anthony Peju had been living in Europe when he was lured by the movie industry to Los Angeles, where he met Herta Behensky, his future wife. Peju established his own nursery, but had long dreamed of owning a farm. The vibrant towns in Napa Valley and their proximity to San Francisco motivated him to begin a search for vineyard property that ended two years later with the acquisition of what would become Peju Province Winery.

Peju's horticultural experience, combined with his wife's talent for gardening, resulted in two acres of immaculately kept winery gardens. Together, they established a dramatic series of outdoor rooms linked by footpaths and punctuated with fountains and marble sculpture. Hundreds of flowering plants and trees create an aromatic retreat for the Pejus and their visitors. Lining both sides of the driveway are forty-foot-tall sycamore trees, their trunks adorned by gnarled spirals. Visitors reach the tasting room by crossing a small bridge over a pool with fountains. An entrance door of Brazilian cherrywood opens onto a naturally lighted room where three muses grace a century-old stained-glass window.

After more than thirty years, Peju remains a small, family-owned winery with two generations working together. Since 2001, elder daughter Lisa has traveled the world representing Peju wines and reaching out to younger customers. Ariana, who joined the team in 2006, has spearheaded such environmental initiatives as installing enough solar panels to provide 35 percent of the energy for the winery (now a Napa Green Certified Winery), earning organic certification at Peju's Rutherford estate, and practicing sustainable farming at the winery's other two properties.

PINE RIDGE VINEYARDS

Located along a viticulturally charmed stretch of the Silverado Trail, in the shadow of Stags Leap Palisades, Pine Ridge Vineyards was founded in a farmhouse in 1978. Just two years earlier, the Judgment of Paris wine tasting had deemed a Cabernet Sauvignon from a neighboring Silverado Trail winery to be superior to its French competitors. That triumph spotlighted Stags Leap District, which was officially recognized as an appellation in 1989.

Pine Ridge has the distinction of owning twelve estate vineyards, totaling two hundred acres, in five of Napa Valley's celebrated appellations, including forty-seven acres in the coveted Stags Leap District. The other appellations are Carneros, Howell Mountain, Oakville, and Rutherford. Where many wineries must rely on purchased fruit to build complexity into their Napa Valley–designated Cabernet Sauvignon, Pine Ridge  has the luxury of selecting from a broad range of estate vineyards located throughout the valley.

Winemaker Michael Beaulac notes that even when crafting nonappellation wine entirely from Cabernet Sauvignon, he faces the welcome challenge of blending from an array of very different estate vineyards. Having formerly consulted on wines sourced from the vineyards of Languedoc-Roussillon and Châteauneuf-du-Pape in France, he understands the elemental truth that wine is not merely made, but is grown in the vineyard.

Tucked among the oak- and pine-clad hills, the winery's simple architecture reflects its farmhouse beginnings. The driveway passes between lawns and pocket gardens offering seating with views of the estate's Stags Leap District vineyards. A rough-hewn pergola shelters a plaque describing the trellising systems displayed in the adjacent demonstration vineyard. Opposite the winery grows one of the few Chardonnay vineyards in Stags Leap District. A hand-stacked rock wall and matching arch mark the boundary of the nearly two-acre block, dubbed Le Petit Clos (the little enclosure).

The tasting room's french doors open onto a carpeted salon with muted colors, partial walls of stone, and a tasting bar of dark Honduran mahogany and polished black granite. Through a glass wall fitted with transparent doors, visitors can see into the original barrel room, a softly lit gallery where wine quietly ages. An additional 4,600 French oak barrels rest in the winery's caves, excavated from solid rock over a period of twenty years. The caves comprise nearly a mile of underground tunnels. At the end of one chamber, cool air, low light, and a display of art glass resembling luminous sea creatures amplify the spirit of a mysterious tropical grotto. Outside the caves, the sun shines on the vineyards, ripening the world-famous fruit of Stags Leap District.

PINE RIDGE VINEYARDS
5901 Silverado Trail
Napa, CA 94558
707-252-9777
800-575-9777
concierge@pineridgewine.com
www.pineridgevineyards.com

OWNER: Crimson Wine Group.

LOCATION: 4 miles southeast of Yountville.

APPELLATION: Stags Leap District.

HOURS: 10:30 A.M.–4:30 P.M. daily.

TASTINGS: $20 for 5 wines; $40 for 5 wines from 5 appellations. 5x5 Tasting, $95, 11 A.M. daily, private tasting of wines from 5 appellations, with small bites (48-hour advance reservation required). Taste on the Terrace, $50 for 5 wines with appetizers (reservation required).

TOURS: Cave walk, barrel tasting, and seated tasting with cheese pairing ($50), daily. Reservation required.

THE WINES: Cabernet Sauvignon, Chardonnay, Merlot.

SPECIALTIES: Appellation-specific estate Cabernet Sauvignon, Fortis (multi-appellation Cabernet Sauvignon).

WINEMAKER: Michael Beaulac.

ANNUAL PRODUCTION: 22,000 cases.

OF SPECIAL NOTE: Garden and terrace for picnics. TGIF wine-and-food pairings on select Fridays spring, summer, and fall. Demonstration vineyard.

NEARBY ATTRACTION: Napa Valley Museum (winemaking displays, art exhibits).

RAYMOND VINEYARDS

RAYMOND VINEYARDS
849 Zinfandel Ln.
St. Helena, CA 94574
707-963-3141
customerservice@
raymondvineyards.com
www.raymondvineyards.
com

OWNER:
Boisset Family Estates.

LOCATION: 2 miles southeast
of St. Helena.

APPELLATION: Rutherford.

HOURS: 10 A.M.–4 P.M. daily.

TASTINGS: Current releases,
$20 for 5 wines; Crystal
Cellar single-vineyard
Cabernet Sauvignons, $25
for 5 wines.

TOURS: $40, includes
Theater of Nature, Crystal
Cellar, and sit-down tasting
of 6 wines. Reservation
required 24 hours in
advance.

THE WINES: Cabernet
Sauvignon, Chardonnay,
Merlot, Sauvignon Blanc.

SPECIALTY: Generations
(Cabernet Sauvignon).

WINEMAKER:
Stephanie Putnam.

ANNUAL PRODUCTION:
200,000 cases.

OF SPECIAL NOTE: Classes on
winemaking, wine-and-
food pairing, and blending
wines by appointment.
Private library tastings by
appointment. Two-acre
demonstration garden with
self-guided tour using on-
site signage or smartphone
audio. Bocce ball court.
Small-lot collection available only in tasting room.

NEARBY ATTRACTIONS: Bothe-
Napa State Park (hiking,
picnicking, horseback rid-
ing, swimming Memorial
Day–Labor Day); Silverado
Museum (Robert Louis
Stevenson memorabilia).

A fantasyland of oenological pleasures awaits visitors who venture inside the ranch-style complex at Raymond Vineyards. With the first glimpse of the dazzling Crystal Cellar, tasters know they've discovered a unique world of sensory surprises, delivered amid dancing neon lights and surreal decor. Entered via a doorway lit by a luminous hologram of a crystal vase, the Crystal Cellar is a working winery, complete with fermentation tanks and a second-story catwalk. When open for tasting, however, the ambience shifts to that of a chic nightclub glittering with candles, Baccarat crystal chandeliers,

and dramatic gleams bouncing off the stainless steel walls and mirror-lined bar. Leggy mannequins clad in faux-fur bikinis pose on the catwalk and dangle from a trapeze with saucy abandon. Servers pouring single-vineyard Cabernet Sauvignon from crystal decanters demonstrate how aeration smooths and softens young red wines by integrating aroma, texture, and flavor. The wild, yet muted lighting creates a magical effect and encourages tasters to rely upon their senses of smell and taste—rather than sight—to experience the wine.

In a side room fitted with reflective stainless steel walls and a spinning mirrored ball, instructional blending sessions take place by appointment. Called the Blending Room, it resembles a spaceship version of a high-tech laboratory. Visitors don futuristic silver lab coats to play mad scientists, and after crafting the perfect Napa Valley blend, they create custom labels for the bottles they will take home. Down the hall, a peek into the members-only Red Room reveals a plush lair decorated in multiple shades of red representing the colors of Cabernet Sauvignon.

Jean-Charles Boisset, whose Boisset Family Estates purchased the winery in 2009, has created a wine lover's playground with a series of interactive attractions. His fun-loving personality is evident throughout the estate and shines in such features as Frenchie Winery, a deluxe five-bed kennel for visiting dogs, and the oversized thronelike chairs set about the lawn for visiting humans. A native of France, Boisset farms his family's Burgundian vineyards using biodynamic practices that emphasize the interplay of soils, plants, and animals. He implemented biodynamic farming at Raymond Vineyards in 2010, when he replanted one-third of the estate's original eighty-one-acre vineyard. The entire ninety-acre estate is farmed according to biodynamic practices and was certified by Demeter in 2013. To illustrate the benefits of this farming method, Boisset created a two-acre demonstration garden called the Theater of Nature. White canvas curtains billow at the entry to the garden, which serves as an outdoor stage for even more sensory surprises and playful pleasures.

ROBERT MONDAVI WINERY

Wineries come and wineries go in Napa Valley, but in this fast-paced, high-stakes world, few can challenge the lasting achievements of the Robert Mondavi Winery. Since its inception more than forty years ago, it has remained in the forefront of innovation, from the use of cold fermentation, stainless steel tanks, and small French oak barrels to the collaboration with NASA employing aerial imaging to reveal the health and vigor of grapevines.

Founder Robert Mondavi's cherished goal of producing wines on a par with the best in the world made his name virtually synonymous with California winemaking. That vision is being carried out today with ambitious programs such as the To Kalon Project. Named after the historic estate vineyard surrounding the winery, this extensive renovation led to the unveiling of the To Kalon Fermentation Cellar, which capitalizes on the natural flow of gravity to transport wine through the production system. Although Robert Mondavi pioneered the use of stainless steel fermentation in the 1960s, To Kalon has returned to traditional oak fermentation, based on the belief that the use of oak enhances the aromas, flavors, and complexity of the winery's reserve, district, and vineyard-designated Cabernet Sauvignon.

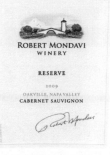

Technological advances aside, the best reason for visiting Robert Mondavi Winery is something less tangible: an opportunity to experience the presentation of wine in the broader context of lifestyle. Educational tours and tastings, concerts, art exhibits, and the industry's first culinary program are all part of the Mondavi legacy. One of the most popular offerings is the Signature Tour and Tasting, which follows the path of the grape from the vine through the cellar to the finished wine. The 550-acre vineyard was named To Kalon (Greek for "the beautiful") by Hamilton Walker Crabb, a winegrowing pioneer who established vineyards here in the late 1800s. It was this property that inspired Robert Mondavi to establish his winery on the site.

Just as the estate's grapes express their *terroir*, the winery itself reflects the location and legacy of Napa Valley. The Spanish mission-style architecture, with its expansive archway and bell tower designed by Clifford May, pays homage to the Franciscan fathers who planted the first grapes in the region. Two long wings project from the open-air lobby to embrace a wide expanse of lawn framed by the Mayacamas Range on the western horizon. Typical of the winery's commitment to the arts, several sculptures by regional artist Beniamino Benvenuto Bufano (who, like Robert Mondavi's family, came from Italy) are displayed in the courtyard and elsewhere around the grounds. In addition, the winery features art exhibits that change every two months.

ROBERT MONDAVI WINERY
7801 Hwy. 29
Oakville, CA 94562
707-968-2000
888-766-6328
info@robertmondavi
winery.com
www.robertmondavi
winery.com

LOCATION: About 10 miles north of the town of Napa.

APPELLATIONS: Oakville, Napa Valley.

HOURS: 10 A.M.–5 P.M. daily.

TASTINGS: $20 for 4 wines in main tasting room; $40 for 4 wines or by the glass in To Kalon Reserve tasting room.

TOURS: Signature Tour and Tasting, including To Kalon Vineyard, by reservation ($25); other tours available seasonally.

THE WINES: Cabernet Sauvignon, Chardonnay, Fumé Blanc, I Block Fumé Blanc, Merlot, Moscato D'Oro, Pinot Noir, To Kalon Cabernet Sauvignon.

SPECIALTIES: Cabernet Sauvignon Reserve and Fumé Blanc Reserve.

WINEMAKER: Genevieve Janssens.

ANNUAL PRODUCTION: 250,000 cases.

OF SPECIAL NOTE: Private cellar tasting and 4-course wine-pairing dinner available with advance reservation. Large shop with wine books and Italian imports. Summer Festival Concert Series (July); Cabernet Sauvignon Reserve Release Party (September).

NEARBY ATTRACTIONS: Culinary Institute of America at Greystone (cooking demonstrations); Napa Valley Museum (winemaking displays, art exhibits).

ROMBAUER VINEYARDS

ROMBAUER VINEYARDS
3522 Silverado Trail
St. Helena, CA 94574
800-622-2206
707-963-5170
www.rombauer.com

OWNER:
Koerner Rombauer.

LOCATION: 1.5 miles north
of Deer Park Rd.

APPELLATION: Napa Valley.

HOURS: 10 A.M.–5 P.M. daily.

TASTINGS: By appointment.
$15.

TOURS: None.

THE WINES: Cabernet
Sauvignon, Chardonnay,
Merlot, Zinfandel.

SPECIALTIES: Diamond
Selection Cabernet
Sauvignon, Joy, Zinfandel
Port.

WINEMAKER: Richie Allen.

ANNUAL PRODUCTION:
80,000 cases.

OF SPECIAL NOTE: Copies
of the latest edition of
The Joy of Cooking and
other cookbooks by Irma
Rombauer are available
in the tasting room.
Zinfandel Port and Joy, a
late-harvest Chardonnay,
available only at winery.

NEARBY ATTRACTIONS:
Culinary Institute of
America at Greystone
(cooking demonstrations);
Bothe-Napa State Park
(hiking, picnicking, horse-
back riding, swimming
Memorial Day–Labor
Day); Silverado Museum
(Robert Louis Stevenson
memorabilia).

The quarter-mile-long drive from the Silverado Trail leads to a winery ensconced in a forest of pine trees. On the far side of the low-slung building, a wide California ranch–style porch affords views that extend to the tree-covered ridge of the Mayacamas Range to the southeast. Without another structure in sight, the serene setting has the ambience of a fairy-tale kingdom secluded from the hustle and bustle of the valley floor. Directly below the winery, a gravel path winds down to a hill where roses are planted in the sun and azaleas thrive in the shade. Scattered about are a half-dozen metal sculptures of fantastical creatures such as a diminutive dinosaur and a life-size winged horse, all weathered to the point that they blend into the landscape.

The Rombauer family traces its heritage to another fertile wine area, the Rheingau region in Germany, where Koerner Rombauer's ancestors made wine. His great-aunt Irma Rombauer wrote the classic book *The Joy of Cooking*. The tradition of linking wine to food is carried on today, with every member of the family involved in the daily operation of the winery, from selecting grapes to marketing the final product. K. R. (Koerner Rombauer III) and his sister, Sheana, are now in charge, respectively, of national sales and public relations.

Koerner Rombauer, a former commercial airline captain, and his late wife, Joan, met and married in Southern California, where both had grown up in an agricultural environment. Since they had always wanted their children to have rural childhood experiences similar to their own, they came to the Napa Valley in search of land. In 1972 they bought fifty acres and settled into a home just up the hill from where the winery sits today. Within a few years, they became partners in a nearby winery. Their hands-on involvement in the winery's operations whetted their appetite for a label of their own and for making handcrafted wines with the passion and commitment of the family tradition. Taking advantage of the topography, the Rombauers built their family winery into the side of the hill. Rombauer Vineyards was completed in 1982.

By the early 1990s, the Rombauers realized they had the perfect location for excavating wine storage caves. Completed in 1997, the double-horseshoe-shaped cellar extends for more than a mile into the hillside. When visitors enter the tasting room, they find a is personalized space with an eclectic assortment of memorabilia from Koerner Rombauer's life. Among the more interesting items are the many signed photographs of famous people as diverse as test pilot Chuck Yeager, entertainer Barbra Streisand, former Secretary of State George Shultz, and country music star Garth Brooks, many of them with personal notes to Rombauer.

RUTHERFORD HILL WINERY

East of the Silverado Trail, a winding mountain road leads to one of Napa Valley's legendary wineries. Here, visitors will find Rutherford Hill Winery, tucked into a hillside and offering a stunning view of the valley. With its gambrel roof and rough-hewn redwood timbers, the winery resembles an antique barn. The impressive building is large enough to house both the winery and the inviting tasting room with its relaxed atmosphere. A pair of gigantic doors greets visitors as they approach the entrance. The winery is framed by expansive lawns and gardens, and a picnic area set in Napa Valley's oldest olive grove.

Rutherford Hill also possesses one of the largest wine-aging cave systems in North America. Begun in 1982 and completed by 1990, the caves are nearly a mile in length. They maintain a natural temperature of fifty-nine degrees Fahrenheit and a relative humidity of 80 percent, conditions that provide the perfect environment and ecologically sensitive way to protect and age the wines. Entering the caves through large doors flanked by towering cypress, visitors immediately notice the heady perfumes of oak and aging Merlot and Cabernet.

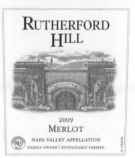

Rutherford Hill Winery was built in 1972 by Joseph Phelps, who soon went on to establish another winery in his own name. In 1976 Bill and Lila Jaeger bought the hilltop property, noting that the region's soils resembled those of Pomerol, a Bordeaux appellation famed for its outstanding Merlot-based wines. The local loam, or "Rutherford dust," a term coined in the late 1930s by famed Russian enologist André Tchelistcheff, is credited with imparting great depth and flavor to the area's plantings of Merlot and Cabernet Sauvignon.

In 1996 Anthony Terlato, a well-known figure in the American fine wine industry, acquired Rutherford Hill with the single-minded goal of producing the finest wines in the Rutherford appellation. Terlato had started his career in his father's Chicago retail wine shop in the 1950s and parlayed a modest business into a leading importer of fine wines. Shortly after purchasing Rutherford Hill, he built a state-of-the-art winery where the winemaker could separately vinify grapes coming from different vineyard lots and grown in many different and idiosyncratic soil types. This allowed the Terlatos and the winemaking team to focus on the specific vineyards producing the finest grapes, including nearly two hundred acres of estate vineyards that are now the foundation of Rutherford Hill wines. Today, Merlot makes up most of the winery's production, underscoring the enduring appeal of wines grown in the renowned Rutherford dust.

RUTHERFORD HILL WINERY
200 Rutherford Hill Rd.
Rutherford, CA 94573
1-800-MERLOT1
707-963-1871
info@rutherfordhill.com
www.rutherfordhill.com

OWNERS: Terlato family.

LOCATION: About 2 miles south of St. Helena, just north of Rutherford Cross Rd. east of Silverado Trail.

APPELLATION: Rutherford.

HOURS: 10 A.M.–5 P.M. daily.

TASTINGS: $15–$30 for 5 wines.

TOURS: Cave and winery tour and tasting. Reservations preferred.

THE WINES: Cabernet Franc, Cabernet Sauvignon, Chardonnay, Malbec, Merlot, Petit Verdot, Port, Sauvignon Blanc.

SPECIALTIES: Merlot, Bordeaux blends.

WINEMAKER: Marisa Taylor Huffaker.

ANNUAL PRODUCTION: 40,000 cases.

OF SPECIAL NOTE: Blend Your Own Merlot hands-on seminar (seasonal). Educational cave tours. Picnic grounds with views (reservations requested). Winery is pet friendly. Reserve and limited-release wines available only in tasting room.

NEARBY ATTRACTIONS: Culinary Institute of America at Greystone (cooking demonstrations); Silverado Museum (Robert Louis Stevenson memorabilia).

SIGNORELLO ESTATE

SIGNORELLO ESTATE
4500 Silverado Trail
Napa, CA 94558
707-255-5990
800-982-4229
info@signorelloestate.com
www.signorelloestate.com

OWNER: Ray Signorello Jr.

LOCATION: 5 miles north of
downtown Napa.

APPELLATION: Napa Valley.

HOURS: 10 A.M.–5 P.M. daily.

TASTINGS: Estate Tasting, $25
for 4 wines; Reserve Tasting,
$35 for 5 wines. Enoteca
Signorello food-and-wine
experience, current and
reserve wines paired with
multicourse bites, $110 for
3 wines, Wednesday–
Sunday, 11:30 A.M. (reservations required).

TOURS: Included with
Enoteca Signorello tasting.

THE WINES: Cabernet Franc,
Cabernet Sauvignon, Char-
donnay, Merlot, Pinot Noir,
Sauvignon Blanc, Semillon,
Syrah, Viognier, Zinfandel.

SPECIALTY: Padrone (red
Bordeaux-style blend).

WINEMAKER: Pierre Birebent;
consulting winemaker:
Luc Morlet.

ANNUAL PRODUCTION:
5,000 cases.

OF SPECIAL NOTE: Epicurean
Summer Series wine-and-
food pairings ($25),
Thursday and Friday, June–
October; Terrazzo Summer
Pairing, with homemade
pizza ($45), Saturday and
Sunday, May–October. Win-
ter cooking classes. Cabernet
Sauvignon, Bordeaux Blanc,
Chardonnay, Pinot Noir,
Syrah, and Zinfandel avail-
able in tasting room only.

NEARBY ATTRACTIONS: Napa
Valley Opera House (live
performances in historic
building); Napa Valley
Museum (winemaking
displays, art exhibits).

Imagine lounging beside a tropical blue infinity pool, while sipping wine and nibbling such delicacies as American Kobe beef and gourmet pizza prepared on-site. Add sweeping views of Napa
Valley and a personal host to pour a diverse lineup of Bordeaux- and Burgundian-style wines,
and the idyllic scene mirrors what you'll find at Signorello Estate. Perched atop a hill, the exquisite
estate resembles a Tuscan-style villa, complete with a terrazzo-tiled terrace, where water bubbles
in a three-tiered fountain and tantalizing aromas drift from a wood-fired pizza oven. Climbing fig
covers the front of the stone-clad winery, tracing a striking geometric pattern. Around the side, a
door opens into the tasting room, called the Enoteca Room, named
for an Italian word meaning "wine repository."

Housed in the former barrel cellar, the 2,000-square-foot Enoteca
Room sports its original ten-foot- tall doors of solid fir. The room was
converted in 2008, when craftsmen hand-troweled plaster onto the walls
and built a copper-topped mahogany bar with faux-marble columns. To
brighten the room, they installed a clerestory window and added
unusual pendant lights made from stiffened copper mesh. A 240-square-foot professional kitchen
in the Enoteca Room lies at the heart of Signorello, an epicurean estate devoted to promoting the
pleasures of matching wine with food. The open kitchen offers clear views of the estate's full-time
chef as he whips up seasonal bites and multicourse meals, often using ingredients from the on-site
garden. Seated tastings are poured in the elegant Enoteca Room and also poolside on the terrace.

Outside, Cabernet Sauvignon and Merlot vines grow on the slope below the pool, and farther
down are five acres of Chardonnay planted by the Signorello family in 1980. The vines are among the
oldest Chardonnay in the region. Additional estate vines grow on the east side of the six-hundred-
foot hill behind the complex. The grapes are hand-harvested and sorted before winemaker Pierre
Birebent, a sixth-generation French winegrower, ferments them using primarily native yeasts.
Birebent crafts the wines according to the Burgundian tradition of the *vigneron*, who strives to grow,
rather than make, the wine.

Winery founder Ray Signorello Sr. purchased the hundred-acre estate in 1977 after retiring
from a career in the petroleum industry. In 1980 he planted forty-two acres of wine grapes and soon
began selling fruit to such renowned wineries as Cakebread Cellars and Caymus Vineyards. In 1985
a bumper crop persuaded Signorello to make his own wine with help from his son, Ray Jr. The two
built the winery in 1986, and after Ray Sr.'s passing in 1998, his son became sole proprietor, director
of winemaking, and the driving force behind this gracious epicurean estate.

SOMERSTON WINE COMPANY

Somerston Wine Company offers visitors a rare opportunity to explore Somerston Estate, a pristine stretch of Napa Valley's rural paradise. Headquartered on a 1,628-acre spread located thirteen miles from St. Helena, the winery hosts a tasting room in downtown Yountville, but encourages oenophiles to head to the country for a singular tasting experience among the vines. At the estate, guests may opt to take an extensive tour of the property, composed of two historic parcels — Elder Valley and Priest Ranch — that have been agriculturally active since the mid-1800s. All visitors, whether or not they join a tour, enjoy a seated tasting of the winery's limited-production Somerston and Priest Ranch wines.

Tours of the estate are conducted in the open-air comfort of an ATV buggy that transports guests through a wonderland with native oaks and wildlife. Highlights include several acres of both ornamental and vegetable gardens, and an island gazebo set in a sparkling lake frequented by swans and ducks. The route winds past acres of terraced vineyards, giving visitors a look at the very source blocks of the three vineyard-designated wines they will taste: Cabernet Sauvignon, Sauvignon Blanc, and a red Bordeaux-style blend called Stornoway. The six Priest Ranch wines are blended from select vineyards to showcase the estate's remarkable diversity, and several of those vineyards are included on the tour.

The journey begins and ends at the winery, located inside a renovated 12,000-square-foot barn equipped with a carbon-neutral cooling, heating, and hot water system. The adjacent tasting room faces an expansive meadow bordered by a Sauvignon Blanc vineyard. A modernist fountain of concrete blocks bubbles on the patio, where staffers pour seated tastings. The tasting room interior has a polished concrete floor and echoes a barrel theme with burnished paneling salvaged from an old redwood barn. The oak tasting bar sports hooplike stainless steel straps across the front. Glass panels provide a long view into the attached barrel room.

Somerston Estate was launched in 2004, when winery co-owner Allan Chapman purchased the 638-acre Priest Ranch, named for the first European to settle the land, in 1849. In 2005 Chapman added the neighboring Elder Valley, 990 acres that included vineyards planted between 1970 and 1999. The estate sustainably farms 225 acres of vines planted in eighty-seven blocks featuring diverse soils, microclimates, and exposures. The spectacularly beautiful vineyards range from 850 to 2,400 feet above sea level, and Somerston Wine Company invites adventurous tasters to visit the idyllic estate, explore the vineyards, and experience the wine at its source.

SOMERSTON ESTATE
3450 Sage Canyon Rd.
St. Helena, CA 94574
707-967-8414
visit@somerstonwineco.com
www.somerstonwineco.com

OWNERS: Allan Chapman, John Wilson, and Craig Becker.

LOCATION: 13 miles east of St. Helena.

APPELLATION: Napa Valley.

HOURS: By appointment.

TASTINGS: $45 for 3 wines. $65 for 3 wines and picnic lunch. One-week advance reservation recommended.

TOURS: ATV buggy tour and a tasting of 3 wines paired with artisan cheeses ($75). One-week advance reservation recommended.

THE WINES: Cabernet Sauvignon, Grenache Blanc, Petite Sirah, Sauvignon Blanc, Zinfandel.

SPECIALTIES: Limited-production wines made from select vineyard blocks; Stornoway (red Bordeaux-style blend).

WINEMAKER: Craig Becker.

ANNUAL PRODUCTION: 5,500 cases.

OF SPECIAL NOTE: Wine tasting on a historic Napa Valley ranch. Occasional cooking classes and wine-maker dinners at the Estate. Somerston Yountville tasting room, 6490 Washington St. (707-944-8200), is open Sunday–Wednesday 1 P.M.–8 P.M., Thursday–Saturday noon–9 P.M. ($20 for 4 current releases). Somerston wines and Priest Ranch Zinfandel, Syrah, and Grenache Blanc available only in tasting room.

NEARBY ATTRACTIONS: Lake Hennessey (boating, fishing, camping); Lake Berryessa (boating, fishing, camping, wildlife watching).

ST. CLEMENT VINEYARDS

ST. CLEMENT VINEYARDS
2867 St. Helena Hwy.
North
St. Helena CA 94574
866-877-5939
www.stclement.com

OWNER:
Treasury Wine Estates.

LOCATION: 3 miles north of
St. Helena on west side of
St. Helena Hwy. North.

APPELLATION: Napa Valley.

HOURS: 11 A.M.–5 P.M.
Wednesday–Monday.

TASTINGS: $25 for choice of
3 tasting menus (including
all-white-wine menu) in
house or on hilltop terrace.

TOURS: By appointment.

THE WINES: Cabernet
Sauvignon, Chardonnay,
Merlot, Rosé, Sauvignon
Blanc.

SPECIALTY: Single-vineyard
Cabernet Sauvignon.

WINEMAKER: Danielle Cyrot.

ANNUAL PRODUCTION:
20,000 cases.

OF SPECIAL NOTE: Picnic
tables overlooking Napa
Valley; box lunch available
with 72-hour notice.
Century-old olive grove.
Winery is pet friendly.
Single-vineyard Cabernet
Sauvignon available in
tasting room only.

NEARBY ATTRACTIONS:
Bothe-Napa State Park
(hiking, picnicking,
horseback riding,
swimming Memorial Day–
Labor Day); Bale Grist
Mill State Historic Park
(water-powered mill circa
1846); Culinary Institute
of America (cooking
demonstrations); Silverado
Museum (Robert Louis
Stevenson memorabilia).

Commanding a hilltop overlooking Napa Valley, the two-story Victorian home of St. Clement Vineyards offers a glimpse of gracious living from a bygone era. Its classic silhouette, complete with front gable, corbeled eaves, and Gothic tower, evokes a storybook destination untouched by time. Along one side, century-old olive trees grow, and on the other, live oaks and flower beds border a lush lawn. Worn stone steps lead up to the house and its wraparound porch, where a wooden swing invites a lazy sojourn. Above the front door, a stained glass transom reveals the home's original address. On an adjacent terrace—one of two outdoor seating areas with the seductive appeal of a rural resort—orange umbrellas and a mature camphor tree shade redwood picnic tables.

Built in 1878, the house was commissioned by a San Francisco glass importer who inaugurated its vinicultural tradition by making wine in the basement. The home sheltered several colorful owners, including a doctor and a pair of somewhat shady sisters, but by 1962 had fallen into disrepair. A real estate investor bought the manse and meticulously restored it, installing period crown molding, light fixtures, and doorknobs. He, too, made wine in the basement. Dr. William Casey, a local ophthalmologist, bought the five-acre property in 1975. He christened the estate St. Clement to honor family ties to Maryland, where a colonial landmark bears the saint's name. From that state's flag comes the cross visible on the label, carved into beams, and set into wrought iron fencing. Casey built a 4,000-square-foot winery behind the house in 1978, using locally quarried stone. With its weathered walls, false gable, and forestlike setting, the building looks like a century-old cellar. Inside, though, it is thoroughly modern, with a lofty platform that gives visitors a bird's-eye view of the work floor.

When Sapporo USA bought the property in 1988, the winery began producing a red wine called Oroppas (Sapporo spelled backward). That offering evolved into St. Clement's flagship wine: a magnificent Cabernet Sauvignon–based blend sourced from select Napa Valley vineyards in the Rutherford, Yountville, Diamond Mountain, Mount Veeder, and Howell Mountain appellations. Over the next decade, the winery changed hands again, and it is now owned by Treasury Wine Estates.

Wines are poured on the terrace, as well as indoors, where the home's original parlor and dining room form the tasting area. Period decor and a convivial atmosphere enhance the feeling of visiting a private home. Guests mingle at two enamel-white bars running the length of the rooms. Six sash windows form a corner bay fitted with cushioned seats that are perfect for relaxing, chatting, and admiring eastward views of Howell Mountain rising above Napa Valley.

STAGS' LEAP WINERY

To visit the Manor House at Stags' Leap Winery is to enter a world of Old California–style wealth, set amid 240 acres of pristine countryside. Like an elegant time capsule, the Romanesque mansion evokes the lavish dinners and lawn parties staged by its builder, San Francisco investor Horace B. Chase. Constructed in 1892 of locally quarried stone, the two-story house stands at the end of a driveway lined with fan palms and the low rock walls of terraced gardens. Mortared stone columns support the roof of a wraparound porch, and a castellated half-turret hosts a massive wisteria vine.

Inside, the gracious home looks as if the family still lives there. Guests are greeted in the sitting room, where sofas bracket a Craftsman-style coffee table and Tiffany lamps glow. Mahogany-hued oak floors, an elaborate staircase, and a carved oak fireplace surround speak of nineteenth-century luxury. After receiving a glass of wine, visitors tour the grounds, which include one of Northern California's first swimming pools. Paths winding among perennial gardens and vegetable beds offer enchanting views of the eighty-acre estate vineyard opposite the house. Following the tour, visitors enjoy a seated tasting in the formal dining room, where soft light filters through Victorian leaded glass windows. The central panel bears the Chase family motto, *Ne cede malis* (Latin for "Yield not to misfortune").

The Chases introduced the Stags' Leap Winery label in 1893, producing wine to sell and share with friends. They took the name from the palisades bordering the property. The Stags Leap Palisades earned the moniker because of a particular rock formation. There, according to legend, indigenous Wappo hunters witnessed a buck magically evade death by vaulting to safety among the crags. The Grange family bought the property in 1913 and turned it into a busy resort. During Prohibition, Mrs. Grange added a speakeasy. The house sat empty from the early 1950s to 1970, when Carl Doumani spent four years restoring it. He revived the Stags' Leap Winery label, and in 1989 the Stags Leap District appellation—sans apostrophe—was recognized. In 1997 the winery was purchased by Beringer Wine Estates, which was acquired by Foster's Group in 2000. A decade later, Foster's stand-alone wine company, Treasury Wine Estates, became the owner of Stags' Leap.

Reaching an elevation of 2,000 feet, the Stags Leap Palisades form a small valley so secluded that even locals rarely venture into it. To find the winery, visitors take an unmarked Silverado Trail turnoff and travel a narrow country road between vineyards, walnut orchards, and private driveways. The effort is worth it, though, for Stags' Leap Winery glimmers with the magic of that mighty buck.

STAGS' LEAP WINERY
6150 Silverado Trail
Napa, CA 94558
800-395-2441
www.stagsleap.com

OWNER: Treasury Wine Estates.

LOCATION: 7 miles north of downtown Napa.

APPELLATION: Stags Leap District.

HOURS: Historical tour and tasting at 10 A.M. and 2:30 P.M. daily. Reservation required; 2 weeks in advance recommended. Maximum of 8 people at a time.

TASTINGS: $55 for 5 wines, tour included. Reservations required.

TOURS: 90-minute historical tour included with tasting. Reservations required.

THE WINES: Cabernet Sauvignon, Chardonnay, Merlot, Petite Sirah, Rosé, Viognier.

SPECIALTIES: Cabernet Sauvignon, Ne Cede Malis (old-vine Petite Sirah blend).

WINEMAKER: Christophe Paubert.

ANNUAL PRODUCTION: 100,000 cases.

OF SPECIAL NOTE: One of Napa Valley's oldest wineries. Historic Manor House built in 1892. Winery is named for Stags Leap Palisades bordering the property; the leap in the legend occurred at a landmark visible behind the Manor House.

NEARBY ATTRACTIONS: Napa Valley Museum (winemaking displays, art exhibits); Napa Valley Opera House (live performances in historic building).

STERLING VINEYARDS

STERLING VINEYARDS
1111 Dunaweal Ln.
Calistoga, CA 94515
707-942-3300
800-726-6136
info@sterlingvineyards.com
www.sterlingvineyards.com

OWNER: Diageo Chateau
and Estate Wines.

LOCATION: 1 mile southeast
of Calistoga.

APPELLATION: Calistoga.

HOURS: 10:30 A.M.– 4:30 P.M.
Monday–Friday; 10 A.M.–
5 P.M. Saturday–Sunday.
Closed major holidays.

TASTINGS: $25 admission
for aerial tram ride,
self-guided tour, 5 wine
tastes, and souvenir glass.
For additional tastings of
reserve and limited-release
wines, visit the website.

TOURS: Self-guided.

THE WINES: Cabernet Franc,
Cabernet Sauvignon,
Chardonnay, Malvasia
Bianca, Merlot, Muscat
Canelli, Petite Sirah, Pinot
Gris, Pinot Noir, Sangiovese,
Sauvignon Blanc, Syrah,
Viognier, Zinfandel.

SPECIALTIES: Merlot, Cabernet
Sauvignon, Platinum
(Bordeaux blend).

WINEMAKER: Harry Hansen.

ANNUAL PRODUCTION:
Not available.

OF SPECIAL NOTE: Display of
Ansel Adams photographs
and wine-related art.

NEARBY ATTRACTIONS:
Silverado Museum
(Robert Louis Stevenson
memorabilia); Napa Valley
Museum (winemaking
displays, art exhibits).

An eye-catching complex of bright white walls and curved bell towers, Sterling Vineyards crowns a forested volcanic knoll three hundred feet above the Napa Valley floor. The winery, which from a distance could double as a hilltop Greek island monastery, commands sweeping views of the geometric vineyards and foothills below. To reach it, visitors leave their cars in the parking lot and board an aerial tramway—the only one of its kind in the valley—for a solar-powered glide over a glistening pond, pines, and live oaks to a walkway among the treetops.

A self-guided tour encourages visitors to explore the stately facility at their own pace, while strategically stationed hosts pour wine samples along the way. Illustrated signboards describe points of interest, and motion-activated flatscreen televisions display videos of winemaking activity. Bells from a former tenth-century London church chime on the quarter hour, their rich tones ringing across exterior footpaths that afford elevated views of the crush pad and fermentation area. Inside the winery, visitors may observe employees at work among stainless steel and redwood tanks, and peek at some of the winery's 25,000 barrels as

they impart delicate flavors to the wine aging within. On the South View Terrace, redwood planters brim with lavender and ornamental grasses, and two sixty-foot-tall Italian cypresses frame the scene to the south. Here, guests sip wine as they take in the panoramic vistas of vineyards, neighboring estates, and parts of the Mayacamas Range on the Sonoma-Napa border, where Mount St. Helena rises above the neighboring peaks to an elevation of 4,343 feet.

Englishman Peter Newton, founder of Sterling Paper International, started the winery in 1964, when he bought a fifty-acre pasture just north of the town of Calistoga. He surprised local vintners by planting Merlot—at the time considered a minor blending grape—along with Chardonnay, Cabernet Sauvignon, and Sauvignon Blanc. Five years later, Newton bottled his first wines, which included California's earliest vintage-dated Merlot. In the early 1980s, the winery purchased one thousand vineyard acres on fourteen different Napa Valley ranches, giving the winemaker a broad spectrum of fruit to work with, as well as control over the farming of the grapes. The winery continues to source fruit from these and two hundred additional acres of select Napa Valley vineyards in various appellations such as Calistoga, St. Helena, Rutherford, and Carneros.

Sterling Vineyards built a reserve wine production facility on the valley floor in 2002, but visitors should make touring the hilltop winery their top priority, as it is one of the most memorable experiences in the Napa Valley.

SUMMERS ESTATE WINES

Calistoga is about as far away as one could get from the high-pressure, high-density world of high finance. Beth and Jim Summers met in that world, when both were working in San Francisco. Earlier, when he was a commercial lender living in New York, Jim had fallen in love with French wines, especially the reds and particularly anything made with Merlot. Over the years, he had visited the California wine country, and by the time he returned to the West Coast, he vowed never to leave again.

Having grown up in Kansas, Jim Summers figured the best way to stay in Northern California was to buy land, and guided by his financial acumen, he figured the most valuable property would be vineyards in Napa Valley.  After some eight years of searching, Summers came upon a wonderful vineyard in Knight's Valley, which is just over the Sonoma County line. In 1987 he purchased the twenty-eight-acre vineyard, which at the time was planted mostly to Merlot and a little Muscat Canelli. Initially, all the grapes were sold to other wineries. The larger than usual harvest of 1993 allowed Summers to produce the first Summers Ranch Merlot—an experience that made him think about all the steps he would have to go through to open his own winery.

After the couple were married, they started looking for a second vineyard. In 1996 they found San Pietra Vara, a winery and tasting room at Highway 128 and Tubbs Lane, about a ten-minute drive from the home ranch. The parcel was an eyesore, but the previous owner had a winery permit and a retail sales permit, so the couple decided to buy it. They transformed the rundown site, preserving the existing wonderful "old vine" Charbono and Zinfandel and replanting the remaining acreage to Cabernet Sauvignon. The Napa Valley property is called Summers Estate Wines; the vineyard designation is Villa Andriana Vineyard, named after their daughter. On the remaining two and a half acres, they installed a hospitality center, a bocce ball court, a picnic area, and a winery and tasting room, which opened in 1997.

The tasting room, which matches the ocher and red color scheme of the adjacent winemaking facility, feels as if it is part of the landscape. Across from the entrance is a horseshoe-shaped tasting bar flanked by french doors that open onto a paved patio with tables and chairs, and a wisteria-covered arbor off to one side. Outside, the eye is immediately drawn to Mount St. Helena and the rugged cliffs known as the Palisades of Calistoga. Some visitors come specifically to sample the winery's signature Charbono, a little-known Italian varietal rarely grown in California.

SUMMERS ESTATE WINES
1171 Tubbs Lane
Calistoga, CA 94515
707-942-5508
info@summerswinery.com
www.summerswinery.com

OWNERS: Jim and Beth Summers.

LOCATION: About 4 miles north of Calistoga via Hwy. 128 or Silverado Trail.

APPELLATIONS: Calistoga, Napa Valley.

HOURS: 10:30 A.M.–4:30 P.M. daily.

TASTINGS: $10 (applicable to wine purchase) for 6 or 7 wines.

TOURS: None.

THE WINES: Cabernet Sauvignon, Charbono, Chardonnay, Checkmate (Bordeaux blend), Merlot, Muscat Canelli, Petite Sirah, Port, Rosé, Zinfandel.

SPECIALTIES: Charbono, Estate vineyards.

WINEMAKER: Ignacio Blancas.

ANNUAL PRODUCTION: 8,000 cases.

OF SPECIAL NOTE: Picnic tables, bocce ball court. Views of Mount St. Helena and of Palisades of Calistoga. Rosé and Muscat Canelli available only in tasting room.

NEARBY ATTRACTIONS: Old Faithful Geyser of California; Robert Louis Stevenson State Park (hiking).

SWANSON VINEYARDS

SWANSON VINEYARDS
1271 Manley Ln.
Rutherford, CA 94573
707-754-4018
salon@swansonvineyards.
com
www.swansonvineyards.
com

OWNER: W. Clarke Swanson.

LOCATION: 200 yards west
of Hwy. 29.

APPELLATIONS: Oakville,
Napa Valley.

HOURS: Wednesday–
Monday, 11 A.M., 1:30 P.M.,
and 4 P.M. (Swanson Salon);
Thursday–Monday 11 A.M.–
4 P.M. (Sip Shoppe). Both by
appointment.

TASTINGS: $20 and up per
flight (Sip Shoppe); $65 for
6 wines plus food pairings
(Swanson Salon).

TOURS: None.

THE WINES: Cabernet
Sauvignon, Chardonnay,
Merlot, Petite Sirah,
Pinot Grigio, Sangiovese,
Sauvignon Blanc, Viognier.

SPECIALTIES: Cabernet
Sauvignon, Merlot, Pinot
Grigio, dessert wines.

WINEMAKER: Chris Phelps.

ANNUAL PRODUCTION:
22,000 cases.

OF SPECIAL NOTE: Clarke's
Bark, custom toffee-
chocolate bar flavored with
the winery's Merlot, and
Alexis Bonbons, made with
dark chocolate and the
winery's Alexis Cabernet
Sauvignon, are sold at the
winery. Small-production
Cabernet Sauvignon and
dessert wines available in
tasting room only.

NEARBY ATTRACTIONS:
Silverado Museum
(Robert Louis Stevenson
memorabilia); Napa Valley
Museum (winemaking
displays, art exhibits);
Culinary Institute of
America at Greystone
(cooking demonstrations).

The redwood gates at Swanson Vineyards swing open as if admitting entry to a private estate. Indeed, the winery's shaded courtyard, terra-cotta-colored walls, and blue shutters give it the look of a villa in rural Provence. Owners Clarke and Elizabeth Swanson enhanced the French theme in 2001, when they built the tasting room and offered the region's first seated, appointment-only tastings. Elizabeth, a New Orleans native, partnered with Bay Area artist Ira Yeager and renowned interior designer Thomas Britt to create a space with the lush textures and features of a bygone era. Called the Swanson Salon, the regal tasting room evokes eighteenth-century Paris so effectively that it feels as if a lively literary gathering might convene at any moment. Displayed on the bright watermelon-hued walls are Yeager's fanciful paintings of eighteenth-century wine vendors. A French stone fireplace provides winter warmth, and a rococo door frame holding a full-length mirror gives the impression of lavish rooms beyond.

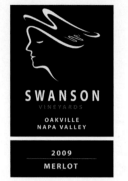

The salonnière greets guests with a glass of wine and seats them around an octagonal Moroccan table inlaid with agates and geodes. Limited to eight people, the tastings are like private dinner parties animated by spirited conversation. The intimate setting invites a leisurely enjoyment of the wines, which are paired with sumptuous small bites, such as aged cheese, tangy fig cake, and potato chips topped with crème fraîche and caviar. To offer a more casual experience, the Swansons opened the Sip Shoppe next door in 2010. Here visitors sample wines amid the festive atmosphere of a circus tent stocked with antiques and eclectic gift items. Red-and-white-striped canvas covers the walls of what staffers hail as a candy store for adults.

The Swansons founded the winery in 1985, the same year they planted wine grapes on a hundred-acre parcel in the Oakville appellation. Although the region was renowned for its Cabernet Sauvignon, the Swansons took the advice of noted winemaker André Tchelistcheff and planted Merlot instead. Agricultural pursuits came naturally to Clarke, whose grandfather operated poultry farms and creameries. Clarke, who graduated from Stanford University in 1961, went on to succeed in banking and as an entrepreneur specializing in radio, cable television, and community newspapers. He was bitten by the wine bug at his twenty-fifth college reunion, when Bob Travers, a former fraternity brother and owner of Mayacamas Vineyards, convinced him to plant grapes in Oakville. Among the first in Napa Valley to bottle Merlot as a stand-alone wine, the family-owned winery ranks as one of the region's premier producers of the variety.

SIP SHOPPE
TASTINGS

GREATEST HITS
PINOT GRIGIO • MERLOT • ALEXIS

SOME LIKE IT RED
SANGIOVESE • ALEXIS • PETITE SIRAH

SOME LIKE IT WHITE
VIOGNIER • PINOT GRIGIO • CHARDONNAY

SOME LIKE IT SWEET
CREPUSCULE • ARIENE • ANGELICA

ENJOY A

TERRA VALENTINE WINERY

Located in a tranquil woodland just fifteen minutes from the bustle of St. Helena, Terra Valentine epitomizes the wonder and diversity of Napa Valley's wineries. The route to the winery winds up Spring Mountain past shadowy redwood groves and seeping springs. As if in a fairy tale, it ends near the peak of the Mayacamas Range in a forest opening where a magnificent stone winery is tucked into a hillside 2,100 feet above Napa Valley. Built on an eighty-acre estate, the two-story, 17,000-square-foot winery resembles a medieval castle, complete with crenellated tower and luminous stained glass windows honoring icons of revelry Bacchus and Dionysus. Pushing open an eight-foot-tall oak door and stepping into the cavelike cellar unleashes a sense of discovery. Inside, a hand-painted Greek-style fresco welcomes Dionysus to "rest your gaze upon this place." Throughout the dimly lit cellar, cast concrete pillars mimic vaulting, and the mottled concrete floor reinforces the impression of great age.

In the foyer, where staffers welcome guests with a glass of wine, towering redwoods are visible through leaded glass windows and matching french doors. While enjoying their first sips, visitors can wander onto a balcony overlooking the estate's Wurtele Vineyard a thousand feet below and the valley floor beyond. The personalized, seated tasting that follows takes place in an elegant drawing room furnished with eighteenth-century oak paneling from a London wine merchant's office.

Erected in the 1960s by a reclusive inventor, the regal winery was in use until the early 1980s, when its builder abandoned it. The building stood empty until Angus and Margaret Wurtele purchased it in 1999. The Minnesota couple named the winery Terra Valentine, combining the Latin word for *earth* with Valentine, Angus's father's name. Four years earlier, the couple acquired a thirty-five-acre vineyard on Spring Mountain Road. Renamed Wurtele Vineyard, it consisted entirely of Cabernet Sauvignon, which would become Terra Valentine's signature wine.

Winemaker Sam Baxter, who worked at Terra Valentine alongside his winemaker father between 1999 and 2002, remembers what he calls the vinicultural "cowboy" days, when the only running water arrived via a spring. The Wurteles cleared trees, paved roads, and replanted the estate's original eight-acre Yverdon Vineyard to Merlot and Cabernet Sauvignon. They restored the winery, installing fifteen automated punch-down fermenters, and opened for visitors in 2003. Three years later, the couple planted the twenty-five-acre Terra Valentine Estate Vineyard to eight different grape varieties, each carefully matched to the soils and microclimates of peaceful Spring Mountain.

TERRA VALENTINE WINERY
3787 Spring Mountain Rd.
St. Helena, CA 94574
707-967-8340
info@terravalentine.com
www.terravalentine.com

OWNERS: Margaret and Angus Wurtele.

LOCATION: 8 miles northwest of St. Helena.

APPELLATION: Spring Mountain District.

HOURS: 10 A.M.–5 P.M. daily, by appointment.

TASTINGS: $30 for 5 wines, with cheese pairing, 10 A.M.–3 P.M. daily, on the hour, by appointment.

TOURS: Winery Tour and Tasting ($30), daily at 10:30 A.M. and 2:30 P.M., with cheese pairing. Estate Tour and Tasting ($75), including vineyard tour and single-vineyard Cabernet Sauvignons paired with artisan cheese. Reservations required.

THE WINES: Cabernet Franc, Cabernet Sauvignon, Merlot, Pinot Noir, Riesling, Sangiovese, Sauvignon Blanc, Syrah.

SPECIALTIES: Single-vineyard estate Cabernet Sauvignon and Marriage (Bordeaux blend).

WINEMAKER: Sam Baxter.

ANNUAL PRODUCTION: 8,000 cases.

OF SPECIAL NOTE: Annual February Valentine's party (check winery website for date and time).

NEARBY ATTRACTIONS: Culinary Institute of America (cooking demonstrations); Bothe-Napa State Park (hiking, picnicking, horseback riding, swimming).

WHITEHALL LANE WINERY

WHITEHALL LANE WINERY
1563 Hwy. 29
St. Helena, CA 94574
800-963-9454
greatwine@
whitehalllane.com
www.whitehalllane.com

OWNER:
Thomas Leonardini Sr.

LOCATION: 2 miles south
of St. Helena.

APPELLATION: Rutherford.

HOURS: 10 A.M.–5:45 P.M.
daily.

TASTINGS: $15 for current
releases; price varies for
reserve selections. No
reservations required.
Seated tastings by
appointment.

TOURS: By appointment.

THE WINES: Cabernet
Sauvignon, Chardonnay,
dessert wine, Merlot, Pinot
Noir, Sauvignon Blanc.

SPECIALTIES: Reserve
Cabernet Sauvignon,
Leonardini Vineyard
Cabernet Sauvignon,
Millennium MM Vineyard
Cabernet Sauvignon.

WINEMAKER: Dean Sylvester.

ANNUAL PRODUCTION:
45,000 cases.

OF SPECIAL NOTE: Limited-
production Leonardini
Family Selection wines
available only at the winery.

NEARBY ATTRACTIONS:
Bothe-Napa State Park
(hiking, picnicking,
horseback riding, swimming
Memorial Day–Labor
Day); Culinary Institute
of America at Greystone
(cooking demonstrations);
Silverado Museum
(Robert Louis Stevenson
memorabilia); Napa Valley
Museum (winemaking
displays, art exhibits).

Ocher and lavender, the colors of a California sunset, soften the geometric lines of Whitehall Lane, an angular, contemporary structure that stands in contrast to the pastoral setting of the vineyard. As if to telegraph the business at hand, the building's large windows have been cut in the shape of wine goblets. In front of the winery, a single row of square pillars runs alongside a walkway, each pillar supporting a vine that has entwined itself in the overhanging pergola.

Glass doors open into a tasting room with a white beamed ceiling, cream walls with black-and-white photos of the vineyard, black counters, and concrete bar tops. The handsome interior befits an estate where the first grapevines were planted in 1880. Even then, Napa Valley settlers were drawn to Rutherford's deep, loamy soils and sunny climate. A vestige of those days, a barn built for equipment storage, is still in use today.

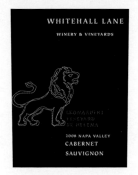

In 1979 two brothers bought the twenty-six-acre vineyard and founded the winery they named after the road that runs along the south border of the property. They produced Merlot and Cabernet Sauvignon before selling the property nine years later. The Leonardini family of San Francisco took over the Whitehall Lane Estate in 1993. Tom Leonardini, already a wine aficionado, had been looking for property to purchase. He was aware of the winery's premium vineyard sources and some of its outstanding wines. Moreover, unlike his previous enterprises, the winery presented an opportunity to create a business that could involve his entire family.

Leonardini updated the winemaking and instituted a new barrel-aging program. He also re-planted the estate vineyard in Merlot and Sauvignon Blanc and began acquiring additional grape sources. Whitehall Lane now owns six Napa Valley vineyards, a total of 125 acres on the valley floor: the Estate Vineyard, the Millennium MM Vineyard, the Bommarito Vineyard, the Leonardini Vine-yard, the Fawn Park Vineyard, and the Oak Glen Vineyard. The various wines produced from these vineyards were rated among the top five in the world on three occasions by *Wine Spectator* magazine.

Whitehall Lane's new building contains a barrel room and a crush pad, as well as a second-floor VIP tasting room. The goal of the facility is not to increase overall production, but to focus on small lots of Pinot Noir as well as wines produced from the St. Helena and Rutherford vineyards. As the winery approaches its thirty-fourth anniversary, the Leonardinis have many reasons to celebrate the success of their family business.

ZD WINES

ZD WINES
8383 Silverado Trail
Napa, CA 94558
800-487-7757
info@zdwines.com
www.zdwines.com

OWNERS: deLeuze family.

LOCATION: About 2.5 miles
south of Zinfandel Ln.

APPELLATION: Rutherford.

HOURS: 10 A.M.–4:30 P.M.
daily.

TASTINGS: $10 for 3 or
4 current releases; $20
for 2 or 3 reserve or older
vintage wines.

TOURS: By appointment.
Cellar Tour: $40; Eco Tour:
$50; Vineyard View: $75.

THE WINES: Cabernet
Sauvignon, Chardonnay,
Pinot Noir.

SPECIALTY: Abacus (solera-
style blend of ZD Reserve
Cabernet Sauvignon).

WINEMAKERS: Robert
deLeuze, wine master;
Chris Pisani, winemaker;
Brandon deLeuze, assistant
winemaker.

ANNUAL PRODUCTION:
30,000 cases.

OF SPECIAL NOTE: Abacus
tasting—comprehensive
tour and tasting of reserve
wines with a focus on
Abacus, $650 for 6 people
minimum.

NEARBY ATTRACTIONS:
Bothe-Napa State Park
(hiking, picnicking,
horseback riding,
swimming Memorial
Day–Labor Day); Silverado
Museum (Robert Louis
Stevenson memorabilia).

Driving along the Silverado Trail through the heart of Napa Valley, travelers are sure to notice the entrance to ZD Wines. A two-ton boulder, extracted from one of ZD's mountain vineyards, is adorned by the winery's striking gold logo, beckoning them to stop for a visit. Crape myrtle trees and rosemary welcome guests as they stroll to the winery entrance. The tasting room provides a cool respite on a hot summer day or a cozy place to linger in front of a fireplace in the winter. Behind the tasting bar are windows that allow visitors to view ZD's aging cellars as they sample ZD Chardonnay, Pinot Noir, and Cabernet Sauvignon.

It has been said that winemaking isn't rocket science, but in fact, founding partner Norman deLeuze had been designing liquid  rocket engines for Aerojet-General in Sacramento when he met his original partner Gino Zepponi. They decided to collaborate on producing classic Pinot Noir and Chardonnay varietals and needed a name for their new enterprise. The aeronautical industry had a quality-control program with the initials ZD, referring to Zero Defects. This matched the partners' initials and created a new association for the letters ZD. In 1969 the winery purchased Pinot Noir grapes from the Winery Lake Vineyard in Carneros in southern Sonoma and produced its first wine, the first ever labeled with the Carneros appellation. Soon after, the winery started making Chardonnay, which continues to be ZD's flagship wine.

Norman deLeuze turned to winemaking full-time, while his wife, Rosa Lee, handled sales and marketing. They purchased six acres, built their own winery, and planted Cabernet Sauvignon in Rutherford in 1979. Four years later, son Robert deLeuze was named winemaker. He had been working in ZD's cellars since he was twelve. In 2001 Robert passed the winemaking reins to Chris Pisani, who had worked closely with Robert for five years, building his appreciation and understanding of the family's consistent winemaking style.

Owned and operated by the deLeuzes for more than four decades, ZD Wines is a testament to the traditions, heritage, and passion of a true family business. Their success in crafting world-class wine has made them one of Napa Valley's iconic families. Founders Norman and Rosa Lee's two sons are currently at the helm of the winery: Robert deLeuze as CEO and wine master and Brett deLeuze as president. Grandchildren Brandon and Jill deLeuze bring in the family's third generation, Brandon as assistant winemaker and Jill handling California sales.

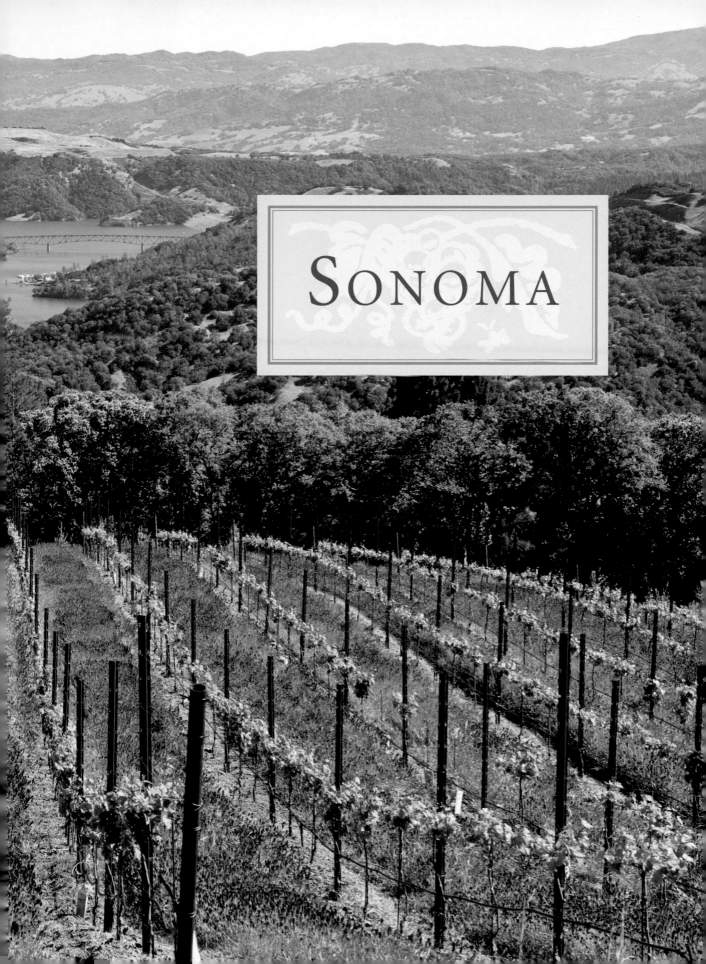

SONOMA

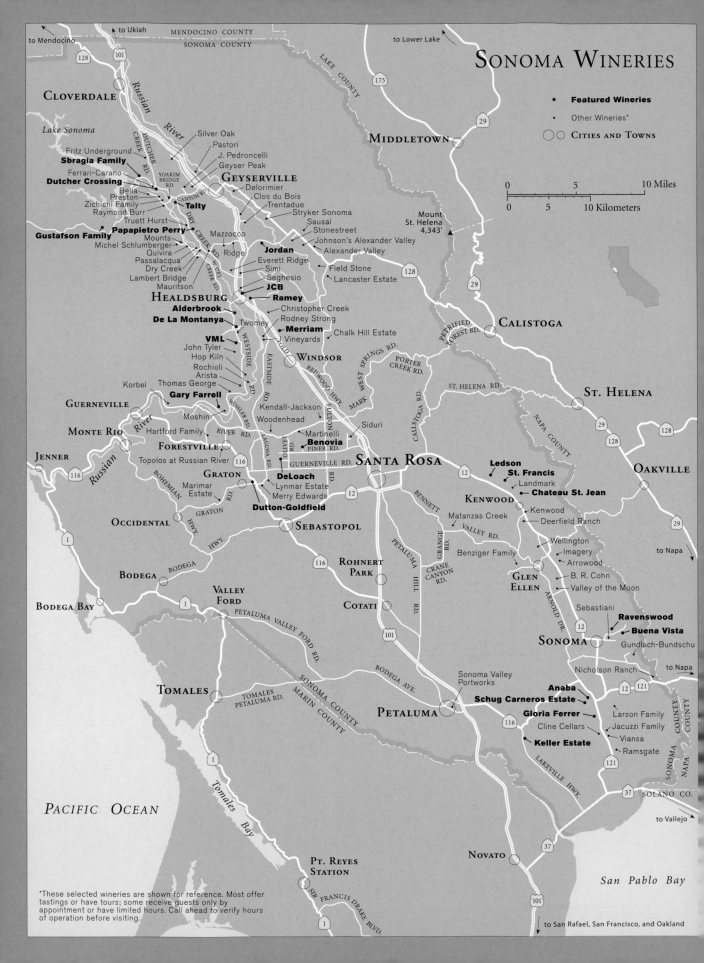

SONOMA WINERIES

- **●** **Featured Wineries**
- **·** Other Wineries*
- **◯◯** **Cities and Towns**

0   5   10 Miles

0   5   10 Kilometers

to Mendocino
to Ukiah
MENDOCINO COUNTY
SONOMA COUNTY
to Lower Lake

CLOVERDALE

Lake Sonoma

LAKE COUNTY

MIDDLETOWN

Russian River

DUTCHER CREEK RD.

Fritz Underground
Sbragia Family
Ferrari-Carano
Dutcher Crossing
Bella
Preston
Zichichi Family
Raymond Burr
Truett Hurst
Gustafson Family
Mounts
Michel Schlumberger
Quivira
Passalacqua
Dry Creek
Lambert Bridge
Mauritson

YOAKIM BRIDGE RD.
CANYON RD.
Talty
DRY CREEK RD.
W. DRY CREEK RD.
Mazzocco
Ridge
Papapietro Perry

Silver Oak
Pastori
J. Pedroncelli
Geyser Peak

GEYSERVILLE
Delorimier
Clos du Bois
Trentadue
Stryker Sonoma
Sausal
Stonestreet
Johnson's Alexander Valley
Alexander Valley

Mount
St. Helena
4,343'

CALISTOGA

PETRIFIED FOREST RD.

Jordan
Everett Ridge
Simi
Seghesio
JCB
Ramey

Field Stone
Lancaster Estate

HEALDSBURG
Alderbrook
De La Montanya
Twomey
VML
John Tyler
Hop Kiln
Rochioli
Arista
Thomas George
Gary Farrell
Korbel
Moshin

Christopher Creek
Rodney Strong
Merriam Vineyards
Chalk Hill Estate

WINDSOR

REDWOOD HWY.
WESTSIDE RD.
EASTSIDE RD.
OLD RD.

ST. HELENA RD.

ST. HELENA

WEST SPRINGS RD.
PORTER CREEK RD.
MARK WEST SPRINGS RD.
CALISTOGA RD.

NAPA COUNTY

128
29
128

GUERNEVILLE

Russian River

MONTE RIO

Hartford Family

JENNER

FORESTVILLE
Topolos at Russian River

GRATON
Marimar Estate

OCCIDENTAL

Kendall-Jackson
Woodenhead
Martinelli
Benovia

Siduri

ROHNER RD.
RIVER RD.
LAGUNA RD.
FULTON RD.
OLIVET RD.
PINER RD.
GUERNEVILLE RD.

SANTA ROSA

DeLoach
Lynmar Estate
Merry Edwards
Dutton-Goldfield

SEBASTOPOL

BOHEMIAN HWY.
GRATON RD.

BODEGA
BODEGA

BODEGA BAY

ROHNERT PARK

COTATI

BENNETT
PETALUMA HILL RD.
GRANGE RD.
CRANE CANYON RD.

Ledson
St. Francis
Landmark
Chateau St. Jean

KENWOOD
Matanzas Creek
Kenwood
Deerfield Ranch
Wellington
Imagery
Arrowood
B. R. Cohn
Valley of the Moon

GLEN ELLEN

VALLEY RD.
ARNOLD DR.

to Napa

Benziger Family

Sebastiani

SONOMA

Ravenswood
Buena Vista
Gundlach-Bundschu

Nicholson Ranch

to Napa

VALLEY FORD

PETALUMA VALLEY FORD RD.

TOMALES

TOMALES PETALUMA RD.
SONOMA COUNTY
MARIN COUNTY

Sonoma Valley Portworks

PETALUMA

BODEGA AVE.

Anaba
Schug Carneros Estate
Gloria Ferrer
Cline Cellars
Keller Estate

Larson Family
Jacuzzi Family
Viansa
Ramsgate

LAKEVILLE HWY.

SONOMA COUNTY
NAPA COUNTY

SOLANO CO.

to Vallejo

PACIFIC OCEAN

Tomales Bay

SIR FRANCIS DRAKE BLVD.

PT. REYES STATION

NOVATO

San Pablo Bay

*These selected wineries are shown for reference. Most offer tastings or have tours; some receive guests only by appointment or have limited hours. Call ahead to verify hours of operation before visiting.

to San Rafael, San Francisco, and Oakland

Sonoma boasts the greatest geographical diversity in California wine country. From the Pacific Coast to the inland valleys, to the Mayacamas Range that defines the eastern border with Napa County, the countryside is crisscrossed by dozens of rural roads, making it an ideal destination for casual exploration.

Most of the county's oldest wineries can be found in the historic town of Sonoma. Facing the extensively landscaped eight-acre central plaza are nineteenth-century adobe and false-front buildings that now house  upscale shops, restaurants, and inns, as well as historic sites.

In the northern part of the county, the city of Healdsburg has recently evolved from a quiet backwater into the hottest destination in Sonoma County. It sits at the hub of three major grape-growing regions—Russian River Valley, Alexander Valley, and Dry Creek Valley—all within a ten-minute drive of the vibrant town plaza.

North of Santa Rosa, the Russian River Valley extends from the Healdsburg area almost all the way to the ocean, where the Sonoma Coast has become one of the most sought-after wine appellations. In addition to the colorful villages clustered along the coastal routes, the region offers boating, swimming, and fishing opportunities and the shade of giant redwoods that soar above the Russian River's banks.

ALDERBROOK VINEYARDS

Healdsburg Plaza, the busy wine, food, and shopping hub of the sophisticated town of the same name, attracts many visitors year-round. But those seeking a peaceful, rural wine-tasting experience in the vicinity can find it less than a mile to the west, at the pastoral Alderbrook Vineyards estate. Sixty acres of vineyards and spacious lawns surround the farmhouse-style tasting room and historic farm buildings—an idyllic setting where visitors can relax, picnic, play bocce ball, and enjoy scenic views of the Mayacamas Range and countryside.

The winery was founded in 1981, when three business partners purchased a former prune orchard and named the site after 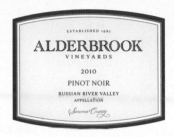 the street on which they lived in Santa Rosa. The property sits at the confluence of Dry Creek Valley and Russian River Valley, and over the years Alderbrook developed a reputation for quality handcrafted small-lot wines from both AVAs. The Terlato family purchased the estate and winery in 2001. To-day, patriarch Anthony Terlato, along with sons Bill and John, manages the family business, which also includes three sister wineries, two in Napa Valley and one north of Santa Ynez.

Winemaker Bryan Parker came to Alderbrook from Pine Ridge Winery in Napa Valley in 2003. Parker sources grapes from the Alderbrook estate vineyards (thirty-eight acres of Zinfandel, seventeen acres of Syrah) and various vineyards in Dry Creek Valley and Russian River Valley. For the Alderbrook label, he crafts six different Zinfandels from Dry Creek, some from single blocks of old vines averaging forty-five to fifty years in age. He also makes Carignane and two Syrahs from Dry Creek Valley, and Pinot Gris, Pinot Noir, and Chardonnay from Russian River Valley fruit. Parker produces wines for a second label, Terlato Family Vineyards, launched in 2005 to focus on food-friendly wines from Napa, Sonoma, and Mendocino counties. These wines include Pinot Grigio, two Syrahs, a Chardonnay, and a Pinot Noir.

In many ways, Alderbrook Vineyards reflects casual life in a country home. Visitors taste wines at a rustic wooden bar under soaring ceilings in an airy, light-filled space containing eclectic displays of gifts for purchase. A lounge area with sofas, armchairs, and a stone fireplace encourages guests to relax and socialize, especially in winter, when a crackling fire warms the room. Visitors can picnic outdoors at tables on the covered wraparound porch and out on sprawling lawns amid colorful gardens. Those who find themselves in Healdsburg Plaza without transportation or who prefer not to drive appreciate Alderbrook's chauffeured pedicab service, with complimentary pickup and drop-off from the square to the rural estate vineyards just a short pedal away.

ALDERBROOK VINEYARDS
2306 Magnolia Dr.
Healdsburg, CA 95448
800-405-5987
info@alderbrook.com
www.alderbrook.com

OWNER: Terlato Family Vineyards.

LOCATION: .5 mi southwest of Hwy. 101 via central Healdsburg exit and Kinley Rd.

APPELLATIONS: Dry Creek Valley, Russian River Valley.

HOURS: 10 A.M.–5 P.M. daily.

TASTINGS: $10 for 5 wines. Groups of 6 or more by appointment.

TOURS: By appointment ($15).

THE WINES: Carignane, Chardonnay, Pinot Grigio, Pinot Gris, Pinot Noir, Port, Syrah, Zinfandel.

SPECIALTIES: Single-block old vine Dry Creek Zinfandels.

WINEMAKER: Bryan Parker.

ANNUAL PRODUCTION: 30,000 cases.

OF SPECIAL NOTE: Live music Sundays 1–4 P.M. seasonally. Bocce ball. Picnic area surrounded by vineyards. Winery is pet friendly. Complimentary pedicab taxi service from Healdsburg Plaza. Annual events include Winter Wineland (January), Barrel Tasting (March), Passport to Dry Creek Valley (April), and Wine & Food Affair (November).

NEARBY ATTRACTIONS: Riverfront Regional Park (hiking, fishing, boating, wildlife viewing); Russian River (swimming, canoeing, kayaking, rafting, fishing); Healdsburg Museum and Historical Society; Hand Fan Museum (collection of antique fans).

ANABA WINES

ANABA WINES
60 Bonneau Rd.
Sonoma, CA 95476
877-990-4188
inquiry@anabawines.com
www.anabawines.com

OWNERS: John and Kathleen
Sweazey.

LOCATION: 4 miles south of
the city of Sonoma at the
intersection of Hwy. 121
and 116.

APPELLATION: Los Carneros.

HOURS: 10:30 A.M.–5:30 P.M.
daily.

TASTINGS: $10 for 5 current
release wines; $15 for 5
single-vineyard wines.

TOURS: By appointment.

THE WINES: Chardonnay,
Grenache, Mourvèdre,
Petite Sirah, Pinot Noir,
Port, Rosé, Syrah, Viognier.

SPECIALTIES: Vineyard-
designated Chardonnay and
Pinot Noir, Rhône-style
blends.

WINEMAKER:
Jennifer Marion.

ANNUAL PRODUCTION:
6,500 cases.

OF SPECIAL NOTE:
Tasting room located in a
100-year-old farmhouse.
Picnicking on a patio
overlooking the vineyard.
Wine available for purchase
by the glass. Port-style
wines, late-harvest Viognier,
and most vineyard-
designated wines available
in tasting room only.

NEARBY ATTRACTIONS:
Mission San Francisco
Solano and other historic
buildings in downtown
Sonoma; Sonoma Raceway
(NASCAR and other
events); biplane flights;
Cornerstone Sonoma
(garden installations by
landscape architects).

Tasters step into history when they visit the Anaba Wines tasting room in a farmhouse built a century ago. A simple structure, it features the high-pitched roof, front gable, and full-width porch typical of California's early rural construction. Fronted by two thirty-foot-tall Canary Island date palms—survivors of the original landscaping—it radiates a powerful sense of place. Nearby, a wind turbine cuts a striking figure against a backdrop of sky and the chaparral-streaked foothills of the Sonoma Mountains. Towering forty-five feet tall, it offers a clue to the meaning of the winery's intriguing name. Anaba (pronounced "anna-bah") derives from the word *anabatic,* which means  "moving upward" and perfectly describes the Carneros appel- lation's climate-defining winds.

When cool breezes off San Pablo Bay, located ten miles south, meet warm mountain slopes inland, they drift upward. The swirling winds drive away fog in the morning and cool the vineyards in the afternoon, which enhances the ripening process. They also spin the turbine's blades, generating clean power for the winery. Owners John and Kathleen Sweazey have taken further steps to run a green operation by sustainably farming the estate vineyards beside the farmhouse. They source additional fruit from vineyards throughout Sonoma County. In each location they meticulously farm their designated blocks. As a result, Anaba boasts an eclectic array of exquisite, small-lot Burgundian and Rhône-style wines. For fans of dessert wines, there are white and red port-style wines, fortified with spirits distilled from estate-grown grapes.

A Chicago native, John discovered wine as a student at Stanford, where he spent weekends exploring Napa and Sonoma counties. After graduating with an economics degree in 1967, he spent nine months in Europe and developed an affinity for the wines of France's Rhône and Burgundy regions. Back in San Francisco, he built a successful real estate finance company and even did a little home winemaking. In 2006 John and Kathleen bought the Carneros property, which included eight acres of vineyards, most of which they replanted to Chardonnay and aromatic whites. Two years later, the couple introduced the Anaba label. They lovingly restored the farmhouse, fashioning the front living area into a tasting room, and opened to the public in 2009.

The room's vintage brick fireplace, open-beam ceiling, and ceramic pitcher full of fresh flowers reinforce the impression of a comfortable country home. Double french doors open onto a spacious redwood deck, where staff often pour seated tastings. The sheltered deck overlooks a lawn bordered by tidy beds of mixed roses, lavender, and ornamental grasses. Beyond the beds grow Chardonnay vines, their leaves gently rustling in the region's signature anabatic breezes.

BENOVIA WINERY

Set on an oak-studded hilltop amid a sea of vineyards in the heart of the Russian River Valley, Benovia Winery's visitor center is just five miles northwest of downtown Santa Rosa. Although it's less than ten minutes from a busy urban center, the fifty-eight-acre estate embodies the pastoral wine country experience typically found in more remote regions of the state. From Highway 101, visitors head away from the Santa Rosa business district, through ranches, vineyards, and orchards, until they spot a small sign marking the entrance to tiny Hartman Road. From there, a half-mile drive leads to a hidden gem: the Benovia visitor center, a two-story ranch house remodeled with sustainable materials and opened to the public in 2012. Panoramic views of vineyards, mountains, and valleys spill from nearly all vantage points at the center, making a secluded setting in which to experience artisanal Sonoma County wines crafted by a native son.

Benovia's story began in 2003, when Joe Anderson and his wife, Mary Dewane, bought the historic Cohn Ranch and legendary vineyard on a ridge above the Russian River. The couple moved to the ranch and decided to dive into the winemaking world, aiming to craft very small lots of premium wines from the best-quality grapes they could obtain — ultimately from their own estate vineyards. They established the winery in 2005 and named it after their fathers, Ben and Novian. In 2005 they acquired Hartman Road Vineyards and Winery from Cecil DeLoach. The couple asked veteran winemaker Mike Sullivan, a Sonoma County native, to join as a partner and lead the winemaking, vineyard development, and management of the winery. The team began upgrading the facilities, adding eco-friendly elements such as solar panels, and planting new vines on the eighteen-acre property. In 2007 Anderson and Dewane purchased a surrounding forty-acre ranch, planted an extensive vineyard, and named it Martaella to honor their mothers (Martha and Eleanor). They also acquired a sixteen-acre site near Freestone. Today Benovia's Sonoma County vineyards total seventy-one acres and are farmed using sustainable and organic practices.

Benovia guests taste the artisanal wines in a rustic, yet elegant setting in the ranch home's former living and dining area, where brightly colored rugs cover floors of earth-friendly bamboo and cork. Visitors gather around an eight-foot African rosewood dining table and compare tasting notes, or relax in soft leather sofas and oversized armchairs by the fireplace. A large room on the second floor displays local art. On fine-weather days, visitors picnic on the shaded decks and patio, where they have an even closer connection with life on a working farm and even more expansive views of Sonoma County wine country.

BENOVIA WINERY
3339 Hartman Rd.
Santa Rosa, CA 95401
707-526-4441
wineryvisits@
benoviawinery.com
www.benovia.com

OWNERS: Joe Anderson, Mary Dewane, and Mike Sullivan.

LOCATION: 5 miles west of downtown Santa Rosa via Fulton Rd. or Bicentennial Way exits on Hwy. 101.

APPELLATION: Russian River Valley.

HOURS: 10 A.M.–4 P.M. daily, by appointment.

TASTINGS: $10. Reservations required.

TOURS: None.

THE WINES: Chardonnay, Pinot Noir, Zinfandel.

SPECIALTY: Small-lot Pinot Noir.

WINEMAKER: Mike Sullivan.

ANNUAL PRODUCTION: 5,000 cases.

OF SPECIAL NOTE: Open house in May and November. Barrel tasting first weekend in March. Cottage overlooking Martaella Vineyards available for rent.

NEARBY ATTRACTIONS: Charles M. Schulz Museum (exhibits on *Peanuts* creator and other cartoonists); Snoopy's Home Ice (ice-skating arena); Sonoma County Museum (regional history and contemporary art and culture); Pacific Coast Air Museum; Luther Burbank Garden and Home (tours of famed horticulturist's property).

BUENA VISTA WINERY

BUENA VISTA WINERY
18000 Old Winery Rd.
Sonoma, CA 95476
800-926-1266
tastingroom@
buenavistawinery.com
www.buenavistawinery.com

OWNER:
Boisset Family Estates.

LOCATION: 2.3 miles east of
the historic Sonoma Plaza.

APPELLATIONS: Los Carneros,
Sonoma Valley, Sonoma
Coast.

HOURS: 10 A.M.–5 P.M. daily.

TASTINGS: $10 for 5 wines.

TOURS: Hour-long tour of
historic caves with Barrel
Tour and Tasting ($30), by
appointment at 11 A.M.

THE WINES: Chardonnay,
Merlot, Pinot Noir,
Sparkling Brut, Zinfandel.

SPECIALTIES: Limited-
production Chardonnay,
Merlot, and Pinot Noir
from Sonoma and Carne-
ros AVAs; wines made from
rare varietals imported
from Europe in the 1860s.

WINEMAKER: Brian
Maloney; consulting wine-
maker: David Ramey.

ANNUAL PRODUCTION:
70,000-plus cases.

OF SPECIAL NOTE: Cheese,
crackers, and wines by
the glass or by the bottle
available for purchase.
Well-stocked gift shop.
Tree-shaded picnic tables.
Winery is family friendly
and pet friendly. Shake-
speare festival in August
and September; historical
play on Saturdays. Vini-
cultural Society wines
available only in the tasting
room.

NEARBY ATTRACTIONS:
Mission San Francisco
Solano and other historic
buildings in downtown
Sonoma.

When Hungarian Count Agoston Haraszthy arrived in California in the 1840s, other pioneers and immigrants were beginning to pour in, lured by the prospect of gold and other opportunities. In 1856 the count, a flamboyant vinicultural pioneer, acquired eight-hundred-acre Buena Vista Ranch in Sonoma and introduced grapevines imported from Europe. Prior to this, the only wine grapes in Sonoma were Mission grapes planted and tended by the Franciscan friars who founded a mission on what is now Sonoma Plaza. In 1857 Haraszthy established Buena Vista Winery, the first premium winery in the state, and built a magnificent home and a massive stone winery with California's first wine caves.

Fast-forward to 2012—when Buena Vista Winery emerged from an extensive renovation of the original winery, caves, and grounds. Boisset Family Estates, which owns other historic wineries, purchased Buena Vista in 2011. Jean-Charles Boisset, president of the family business, had visited Buena Vista on his first trip to California when he was eleven years old. The deep sense of history, the stone buildings, and the verdant setting made an indelible impression. Later, after settling in Napa, he pounced on the opportunity to acquire the historic winery and surrounding property. Boisset, whose passion for California wines and pioneering spirit are often compared with Count Haraszthy's, immediately launched plans to restore the estate to its former glory while adding twenty-first-century equipment for crafting premium wines.

The 2012 harvest marked the first vintage to be made in the historic cellars in decades. Wine-makers Brian Maloney and David Ramey oversee wine production, which includes five collections. The Sonoma and Carneros wines are sourced from grapes within these two appellations. Vinicultural Society wines use esoteric, historical varietals originally imported by the count from 1861 to 1863. The Count showcases a limited-production red wine for the vintage, and the Private Reserve features the top-tier wines.

A visit to Buena Vista, only two miles from bustling downtown Sonoma, is a rare chance to experience firsthand California's rich winemaking heritage and Buena Vista's storied past. The fully restored buildings (on both state and national registers of historic places) and grounds include cobblestone terraces, a vortex fountain, a demonstration vineyard with examples of original vines the count brought from Europe, and a heritage garden with fruits and vegetables grown in the Americas. Guests taste wines in the two-story historic stone press house, which holds fascinating exhibits about Count Haraszthy and Buena Vista Winery's 150-year-old tale.

CHATEAU ST. JEAN WINERY

With the dramatic profile of Sugarloaf Ridge as a backdrop, the exquisitely landscaped grounds at Chateau St. Jean Winery in Kenwood evoke the image of a grand country estate. The château itself dates to the 1920s, but it wasn't until 1973 that a family of Central Valley, California, growers of table grapes founded the winery. They named it after a favorite relative and, with tongue in cheek, placed a statue of "St. Jean" in the garden.

The winery building was constructed from the ground up to suit Chateau St. Jean's particular style of winemaking. The founders believed in the European practice of creating vineyard-designated wines, so they designed the winery to accommodate numerous lots of grapes, which could be kept separate throughout the winemaking process. Wines from each special vineyard are also bottled and marketed separately, with the vineyard name on the label. The winery makes a dozen vineyard-designated wines from the Sonoma Valley, Alexander Valley, Russian River Valley, and Carneros appellations. The winery also produces other premium varietals and one famously successful blend, the flagship Cinq Cépages Cabernet Sauvignon.

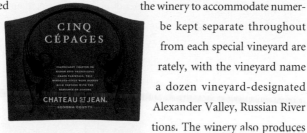

Chateau St. Jean became the first Sonoma winery to be awarded the prestigious Wine of the Year award from *Wine Spectator* magazine for its 1996 Cinq Cépages, a Bordeaux-style blend of five varieties, including Cabernet Sauvignon, Cabernet Franc, and Malbec. The winery received high acclaim again when it was given the #2 Wine of the Year award from *Wine Spectator* for its 1999 Cinq Cépages Cabernet Sauvignon. Winemaker Margo Van Staaveren has nearly thirty years of vineyard and winemaking experience with Chateau St. Jean, and her knowledge of Sonoma further underscores her excellence in highlighting the best of each vineyard.

In the summer of 2000, Chateau St. Jean opened the doors to its new Visitor Center and Gardens. A formal Mediterranean-style garden contains roses, herbs, and citrus trees planted in oversized terra-cotta urns arranged to create a number of open-air "rooms." Visitors have always been welcome to relax on the winery's redwood-studded grounds, but now the setting is enhanced by the extensive plantings, making the one-acre garden attractive throughout the year.

Beyond the Mediterranean garden is the tasting room with a custom-made tasting bar. Fashioned from mahogany with ebony accents, the thirty-five-foot-long bar is topped with sheet zinc. The elegant château houses the Reserve Tasting Room. Visitors who would like to learn more about Chateau St. Jean wines are encouraged to make a reservation for a more in-depth program.

CHATEAU ST. JEAN WINERY
8555 Hwy. 12
Kenwood, CA 95452
877-478-5326
www.chateaustjean.com

OWNER: Treasury Wine Estates.

LOCATION: 8 miles east of Santa Rosa.

APPELLATION: Sonoma Valley.

HOURS: 10 A.M.–5 P.M. daily, except major holidays.

TASTINGS: $15 in main Tasting Room; $25 in Reserve Tasting Room.

TOURS: Promenade Tour available, weather permitting. Visit www.chateaustjean.com for further information.

THE WINES: Cabernet Franc, Cabernet Sauvignon, Chardonnay, Fumé Blanc, Gewürztraminer, Malbec, Merlot, Pinot Blanc, Pinot Noir, Riesling, Syrah, Viognier.

SPECIALTIES: Cinq Cépages and vineyard-designated wines.

WINEMAKER: Margo Van Staaveren.

ANNUAL PRODUCTION: 400,000 cases.

OF SPECIAL NOTE: Picnic tables in oak and redwood grove. Wine education classes. Open houses on most holidays. Store offering gourmet food and merchandise.

NEARBY ATTRACTION: Sugarloaf Ridge State Park (hiking, camping, horseback riding).

DE LA MONTANYA WINERY & VINEYARDS

DE LA MONTANYA WINERY & VINEYARDS
999 Foreman Ln.
Healdsburg, CA 95448
707-433-3711
dennis@dlmwine.com
www.dlmwine.com

OWNERS: Dennis and Tina De La Montanya.

LOCATION: 3 miles southwest of Healdsburg.

APPELLATIONS: Sonoma Coast, Russian River Valley, Dry Creek Valley, Alexander Valley, Clear Lake.

HOURS: 11 A.M.–5 P.M. daily.

TASTINGS: $10 for 6–10 wines (applicable to purchase).

TOURS: None.

THE WINES: Cabernet Sauvignon, Chardonnay, Gewürztraminer, Merlot, Petite Sirah, Pinot Noir, Sauvignon Blanc, Tempranillo, Viognier, Zinfandel.

SPECIALTIES: Vineyard-driven, small-lot wines.

WINEMAKER: Tami Collins.

ANNUAL PRODUCTION: 5,000 cases.

OF SPECIAL NOTE: Wines are 90 percent estate grown and available in tasting room only. Large informal garden and picnic area with bocce ball and horseshoe pit. Winery is pet friendly.

NEARBY ATTRACTIONS: Russian River (swimming, canoeing, kayaking, rafting, fishing); Lake Sonoma (hiking, fishing, boating, camping, swimming).

The road to De La Montanya Winery curves past the vineyards of Dry Creek Valley, through woods, and under a rural bridge before arriving at the winery's understated entrance. Although just a few yards from busy Westside Road, the quiet spot feels more like a hidden retreat than part of an active wine trail. Old barrels and farm equipment dotting informal flower beds, and the barnlike winery, with its monitor roof and board-and-batten redwood siding, enhance the farmyard flavor.

On one side of the winery, a simple door of knotty alder opens into the tasting room, a small space alive with a country-kitchen friendliness. Lighthearted banter and the occasional wisecrack can be heard from both staff and visitors. Faux antique hutches display bottled wine, and double doors with large glass panes offer a view into the attached winery and barrel room. Tasters gather at the curved, Brazilian granite bar or head out to the patio, where seated tastings are poured on busy days. Zinfandel vines grow within a few feet of the patio, which has umbrella-shaded tables and a wood-fired pizza oven. Bordering the intimate

space are beds of lavender, roses, and crape myrtle. A concrete path lined with tree roses and Zinfandel vines leads to a garden wonderland, where visitors can relax. As inviting as a comfortable backyard, the lawn is set with redwood picnic tables. Nearby, a bocce ball court and horseshoe pit are ready for play. Golden Delicious apple trees remaining from a 1950s-era orchard edge the grass.

Over the decades, Dry Creek Valley farmers have grown a variety of crops, from grapes in the late 1800s to walnuts, plums, apples, and, fueled by the 1970s wine boom, grapes again. Dennis De La Montanya decided to join their ranks in 1988, when a real estate appraisal he did alerted him to the value of wine grapes. Applying his experience in both banking and real estate sales, he started buying land with wine grapes in mind. He planted his first vineyard in 1994 and crafted his debut vintage, a Viognier, four years later.

De La Montanya currently farms 270 acres spanning five appellations: Sonoma Coast, Russian River Valley, Dry Creek Valley, Alexander Valley, and Clear Lake. He bottles eighteen different wines, some in lots as small as twenty-four cases. His popular Pin-Up series of red blends features labels bearing playfully provocative photographs of wine club members. A descendant of French Huguenots who settled New Amsterdam in 1637, De La Montanya grew up on a cattle ranch in Marin County. He is a sixth-generation Californian who produces refined wines, while infusing a bit of the rambunctious West into his cheerful tasting room.

DeLoach Vineyards

As visitors step along a brick terrace leading to the DeLoach Vineyards tasting room, they pass a twenty-foot-high wooden sculpture of an ethereal woman reaching toward the sky and holding a child in the palm of her hand. The work, titled *Earth and Sky*, embodies DeLoach's dedication to biodynamic farming principles and environmental stewardship. The twenty-five-acre farm in the western Russian River Valley received organic certification in 2008 from the California Certified Organic Farmers and biodynamic certification in 2009 from Demeter. Today the estate teems with life, in the vineyards and in a half-acre biodynamic garden where lavender and other fragrant plants scent the air.

Although DeLoach is one of the region's oldest vineyards, its sustainable practices are relatively new. Pioneering winemaker Cecil DeLoach planted Pinot Noir vines here in 1973 and helped establish the Russian River Valley AVA. For decades, DeLoach enjoyed a widespread reputation for excellent Pinot Noir, Chardonnay, and Zinfandel production. In the early 2000s, French wine entrepreneur Jean-Charles Boisset toured the Russian River Valley for the first time and instantly recognized the region's potential to create Pinot Noir wines to rival those from his native Burgundy. Boisset Family Estates purchased DeLoach Vineyards in 2003. A passionate protector of the environment, Boisset quickly began to transform the estate. After the 2004 vintage, he removed existing vineyards and replanted them with cover crops designed to revitalize the soil. Two years later, he planted new vines. During the transition period, the winery sourced grapes from other eco-minded growers in the region. Then, in 2011 the winery released its first vintage made exclusively from estate grapes farmed with biodynamic techniques.

DeLoach's environmental innovations extend to green packaging, including its popular Barrel-to-Barrel container system. Wine is stored in three-liter eco-bags, housed in a recyclable cardboard box that protects the wine from oxidation for up to six weeks. The replaceable bag and box fit inside an oak barrel with a spigot for individual glass pours. This system eliminates corkage, reduces packaging by 99 percent compared to glass, and requires less energy to transport.

DeLoach's tasting room evokes rustic, laid-back Sonoma County but with a luxurious touch. Guests sample limited-release, vineyard-designated wines at the composite-stone bar or at picnic tables on the terrace. Tours of the vineyards and biodynamic garden enable visitors to extend their experience beyond the tasting room, in a vibrant Russian River Valley ecosystem.

DeLoach Vineyards
1791 Olivet Rd.
Santa Rosa, CA 95401
707-526-9111 ext. 109
winestore@
deloachvineyards.com
www.deloachvineyards.
com

Owner:
Boisset Family Estates.

Location: On Olivet Rd. between River Rd. and Guerneville Rd.

Appellation: Russian River Valley.

Hours: 10 A.M.–5 P.M. daily.

Tastings: $10 for 5 wines; Pinot Experience reserve tasting by appointment, $30 for 5 wines (includes barrel tasting). Taste of Terroir, $50, seated private tasting of Burgundian wines in guesthouse, by appointment.

Tours: Daily at 11 A.M. ($15); no appointment required.

The Wines: Chardonnay, Pinot Noir, Pinot Noir Rosé, Zinfandel.

Specialties: Vineyard-designated Pinot Noirs.

Winemaker: Brian Maloney; consulting winemaker: Dan Goldfield.

Annual Production: 175,000 cases.

Of Special Note: Picnic areas in a courtyard and in other locations on the grounds. Deli foods available for purchase; cheese platters available with advance notice. Complimentary food-and-wine pairings first Saturday and Sunday of the month. Winery is pet friendly.

Nearby Attraction: Charles M. Schulz Museum (exhibits on *Peanuts* creator and other cartoonists).

DUTCHER CROSSING WINERY

DUTCHER CROSSING WINERY
8533 Dry Creek Rd.
Geyserville, CA 95441
707-431-2700
866-431-2711
info@dutchercrossing
winery.com
www.dutchercrossing
winery.com

OWNER: Debra Mathy.

LOCATION: 8.5 miles west of
Dry Creek Valley exit off
U.S. 101 via Dry Creek Rd.

APPELLATION: Dry Creek
Valley.

HOURS: 11 A.M.–5 P.M. daily.

TASTINGS: $5 for 4-wine
flight; $10 for reserve wine
flight.

TOURS: ATV vineyard tours
by appointment.

THE WINES: Cabernet
Sauvignon, Chardonnay,
Merlot, Petite Sirah, Port,
Sauvignon Blanc, Syrah,
Zinfandel.

SPECIALTY: Cabernet
Sauvignon blend.

WINEMAKER:
Kerry Damskey.

ANNUAL PRODUCTION:
7,000 cases.

OF SPECIAL NOTE: Picnic
tables (reservations for
parties of six or more) and
pétanque court; limited
deli selections available.
Select wines sold only at
tasting room.

NEARBY ATTRACTION:
Lake Sonoma (swimming,
fishing, boating, hiking,
camping).

utcher Crossing Winery exemplifies the low-key ambience of Dry Creek Valley, an appellation sixteen miles long and at most two miles across that has been home to generations of grape growers and winemakers. Sited at a scenic junction of two creeks — Dry Creek and Dutcher Creek — the small winery has a quaint charm, and its architecture evokes the look of the farming community that first flourished here in the early 1900s. A wide breezeway between the tasting room and the winemaking building offers panoramic views of the valley's hillside beauty.

Purchased by Debra Mathy in 2007, Dutcher Crossing produces small-lot, vineyard-designated wines crafted by winemaker Kerry Damskey. In addition to the signature Cabernet Sauvignon–Syrah blend, he makes several Dry Creek Valley Zinfandels, select Chardonnays from the Alexander Valley, and Pinot Noir sourced from the Russian River Valley. Over his thirty years as a winemaker, Damskey has become a leading proponent of blending; his Cabernet Sauvignon–Syrah is the first wine of its kind in Dry Creek Valley.

Proprietor Mathy expressed her adventuresome side by planting an estate vineyard block in the Châteauneuf-du-Pape style: a selection of Rhône varieties such as Grenache, Syrah, Mourvèdre, Cinsault, and Counoise. Guests can sip their selections while overlooking this planting from the trellised picnic area, set amid colorful gardens. Views of the valley landscape are also visible through the tall windows in the spacious tasting room, where highlights include a vaulted beam ceiling, a polished limestone tasting bar, and wide hickory plank floors. At one end of the rectangular room, a cozy conversation area with comfortable seating faces a fireplace made from locally quarried stone and topped with a mantel fashioned from distressed railroad ties. A vintage bicycle, the icon chosen to grace the redesigned Dutcher Crossing wine label, is also on display. It is a replica of an 1892 Rudge crafted in the classic Penny Farthing style so that the front wheel is larger than the back.

Debra Mathy considers the bicycle a symbol of the timeless qualities of an artisan approach to life as well as to winemaking. As the last Christmas present she received from her late father, it also represents her journey to find Dutcher Crossing Winery. Mathy, an avid cyclist and lover of bicycles since childhood, spent ten years traveling with her father to discover the winery of their dreams. She can almost always be found during the day greeting visitors, with her golden lab, Dutchess, at her side. Their friendliness and enthusiasm reflect the culture and spirit of Dutcher Crossing.

DUTTON-GOLDFIELD WINERY

Dutton-Goldfield Winery was born in 1998, when longtime friends Steve Dutton and Dan Goldfield shook hands in a historic vineyard on the western edge of the Russian River Valley. In the early 1960s, many people considered this region too cool for growing premium wine grapes, but at the time, fourth-generation farmer Warren Dutton, Steve's father, aimed to prove otherwise. The Dutton family had grown pears, hops, apples, and other crops in the Santa Rosa area since the 1880s. Dutton had a hunch that the cool-climate western Russian River Valley held excellent grape-growing potential. He ignored the naysayers and in 1964, with his wife, Gail, purchased thirty-five acres just west of the tiny town of Graton, located northwest of Sebastopol. He built a home and planted Chardonnay vines, hoping they would thrive close to cool Pacific breezes.

The vineyard became a success, and Warren Dutton's experiment encouraged many other pioneering growers to plant wine grapes in the area. Dutton Ranch gradually acquired additional land and today includes more than 1,100 acres of grapes and 200 acres of organically farmed apples. Steve Dutton, his brother, Joe, and their mother, Gail, collectively operate the family business. Steve oversees the original Chardonnay vineyard and more than sixty additional plots of Chardonnay, Pinot Noir, Syrah, and Zinfandel in the Russian River Valley, Green Valley, and Sonoma Coast appellations. Many respected wineries purchase Dutton Ranch grapes to produce much-lauded Chardonnay.

The 1998 handshake marked a promising venture for Dutton Ranch—the union of Steve Dutton's extensive grape-growing expertise with Dan Goldfield's experience in the winemaking business. After Goldfield graduated from Brandeis University, he headed to California to pursue a career as a research chemist. Out west he discovered a passion for Burgundian wines and decided to switch careers. He earned a master's in enology from UC Davis in 1986, then worked at Napa Valley wineries and spent two years in Portugal learning on the job. He subsequently honed specialized skills in crafting Pinot Noir and Chardonnay as winemaker at Sonoma County's La Crema Winery and Hartford Court. When the opportunity arose to team up with Steve Dutton, Goldfield jumped at the chance to make single-vineyard-designated wines sourced from a wide range of vineyards.

The Dutton-Goldfield tasting room, opened in 2010, occupies the front section of the spacious winery facility in the quaint village of Graton, near the Duttons' historic Chardonnay vineyard. The casual vibe and simple furnishings enable guests to focus on the wines, poured at a curved laminate bar. Visitors listen to music while lounging indoors by the fireplace or outdoors on the patio.

DUTTON-GOLDFIELD WINERY
3100 Gravenstein Hwy. North
Sebastopol, CA 95472
707-827-3600
info@duttongoldfield.com
www.duttongoldfield.com

OWNERS: Steve Dutton and Dan Goldfield.

LOCATION: Northwest corner of intersection of Hwy. 116 (Gravenstein Hwy.) and Graton Rd.

APPELLATION: Russian River Valley.

HOURS: 10 A.M.–4:30 P.M. daily.

TASTINGS: Complimentary with wine purchase, otherwise $15. Groups of 6 or more by appointment.

TOURS: None.

THE WINES: Chardonnay, Gewürztraminer, Pinot Blanc, Pinot Noir, Syrah, Zinfandel.

SPECIALTIES: Single-vineyard-designated Pinot Noir and Chardonnay.

WINEMAKER: Dan Goldfield.

ANNUAL PRODUCTION: 10,000 cases.

OF SPECIAL NOTE: Enclosed patio with tables and chairs. Live music every Sunday afternoon May–October. Rotating displays of local art. Jars filled with cinnamon, cardamom, and other aromatic ingredients help visitors identify a wine's tasting notes.

NEARBY ATTRACTIONS: Russian River (swimming, canoeing, kayaking, rafting, fishing); Armstrong Woods State Natural Reserve (hiking, horseback riding); Sonoma Canopy Tours (zipline and eco-tours of redwoods).

GARY FARRELL VINEYARDS AND WINERY

GARY FARRELL VINEYARDS AND WINERY
10701 Westside Rd.
Healdsburg, CA 95448
707-473-2909
concierge@
garyfarrellwinery.com
www.garyfarrellwinery.com

FOUNDER: Gary Farrell.

LOCATION: 12 miles
southwest of downtown
Healdsburg.

APPELLATION: Russian River
Valley.

HOURS: 10:30 A.M.–
4:30 P.M. daily.

TASTINGS: $15 for
5 single-vineyard wines.
Terrace (summer) and
Fireside (winter) seated
tastings, $25 for 5 or
6 single-vineyard and
limited-production wines.
Reservations recommended
for seated tastings.

TOURS: 10:30 A.M. daily
($35), seated tasting
included. Reservations
required.

THE WINES: Chardonnay,
Pinot Noir, Sauvignon
Blanc, Syrah, Zinfandel.

SPECIALTIES: Vineyard-
designated Chardonnay
and Pinot Noir.

WINEMAKER:
Theresa Heredia.

ANNUAL PRODUCTION:
17,000 cases.

OF SPECIAL NOTE: Original
art by local artists for
purchase in tasting room.
Sweeping views of Russian
River Valley. Featured
wines available in the
tasting room only.

NEARBY ATTRACTIONS:
Russian River (rafting,
fishing, swimming,
canoeing, kayaking);
Armstrong Redwoods
State Natural Reserve
(hiking, horseback riding).

Meandering Westside Road traces the course of the Russian River through aromatic redwood groves and past some of the region's oldest and most prestigious vineyards. The northern end of Westside, closer to Healdsburg, is lined with wineries, but down near Wohler Avenue, on the outskirts of leafy Forestville, most structures are likely to be residences. There is little to prepare travelers for the dramatic entrance to Gary Farrell Winery, where a sharp turn leads up a steep driveway that climbs past native live oaks and a dramatic stand of towering redwoods.

Winery founder Gary Farrell opened his eponymous facility in 2000, high on a ridge overlooking a bewitching slice of the  Russian River appellation, famed for outstanding Pinot Noir and Chardonnay. Farrell made his first vintage in 1982, producing fifty cases of Pinot Noir from the nearby Rochioli and Allen vineyards, two highly regarded estates. He was among the first to recognize the world-class potential of Russian River Valley fruit. In the early 1980s, most area grapes disappeared into nameless blends, but when Farrell, along with such local pioneers as Davis Bynum, Joe Rochioli, and Tom Dehlinger, started making stellar wine, they ignited the region's fame. Farrell forged lasting relationships with like-minded visionaries. As a result, thirty years on, the winery has access to fruit from some of the region's most coveted vineyards, including Rochioli, Bacigalupi, and Ritchie.

Located well off the beaten path, the winery sits at an elevation of four hundred feet, but the steep slopes create the illusion of a much higher vantage point. Visitors enter the winery beneath a sculptural redwood arbor, and about two steps inside the tasting room, they are likely to simply stop and gape at the sweeping vista of madrones, valley oaks, and redwoods visible through wall-to-wall picture windows behind the tasting bar. The ambience is woodsy yet refined, with little to distract from experiencing the wines, which are small-production, single-vineyard Pinot Noir and Chardonnay that epitomize the best of the Russian River Valley appellation.

Tastings range from a casual sampling at the bar to a hosted, seated experience that often includes one or two library pours. All take place in view of the redwoods that define this part of the world, where ribbons of fog can often be seen drifting through the forested valley below. Here, close to the wines' source, visitors are imbued with a visceral memory of how the Russian River Valley influences the wine in the glass.

GLORIA FERRER CAVES & VINEYARDS

The Carneros appellation, with its continual winds and cool marine air, is known far and wide as an ideal climate for growing Pinot Noir and Chardonnay grapes. The word spread all the way to Spain, where the Ferrer family had been making sparkling wine for more than a century. The Ferrers are the world's largest producer of sparkling wine.

Members of the family had been looking for vineyard land in the United States off and on for fifty years when José and Gloria Ferrer visited the southern part of the Sonoma Valley. The climate reminded them of their Catalan home in Spain, and in 1982 they acquired a forty-acre pasture and then, four years later, another two hundred acres nearby. They started planting vineyards with Pinot Noir and Chardonnay, the traditional sparkling wine grapes. The winery now cultivates nearly four hundred acres in Carneros and, in addition to sparkling wines, produces still wines, including Pinot Noir, Merlot, and Chardonnay. Gloria Ferrer wines have a history of critical success. Within a year of its 1986 debut, the winery won seven gold medals, marking the beginning of many accolades to come. Since the winery opened, the wines have received more than 700 gold medals.

The winery that José Ferrer built was the first sparkling wine house in Carneros. Named for his wife, it was designed after a *masia* (a Catalan farmhouse), complete with terraces, a red tile roof, and thick walls the color of the Spanish plains. Complementing the exterior, the winery's cool interior has tile floors and Spanish antiques. The ties to Spain continue in the winery's shop, which offers a selection of cookbooks devoted to Spanish cuisine and the specialties of Catalonia. Also available are several Sonoma-grown products such as Gloria Ferrer's sparkling wine–filled chocolates, and both local and Spanish cheeses, as well as other Spanish delicacies.

Visitors are welcome to enjoy Gloria Ferrer wines, both still and sparkling, in the spacious tasting room or outside on the Vista Terrace. There they are treated to a breathtaking view of Carneros and the upper reaches of San Pablo Bay. On a clear day, they can see all the way to the peak of 3,848-foot Mount Diablo in the East Bay. Both still and sparkling wines are aged in the caves tunneled into the hill behind the visitor center.

Tours of the winery include a visit to these aromatic dark recesses, where guides explain the traditional *méthode champenoise* process of creating sparkling wine, during which the wine undergoes its secondary fermentation in the bottle — the one that forms the characteristic bubbles.

GLORIA FERRER CAVES & VINEYARDS
23555 Hwy. 121
Sonoma, CA 95476
707-933-1917
info@gloriaferrer.com
www.gloriaferrer.com

OWNERS: Ferrer family.

LOCATION: 4 miles south of the town of Sonoma.

APPELLATION: Los Carneros.

HOURS: 10 A.M.–5 P.M. daily.

TASTINGS: $6–$14 per glass of sparkling wine; $3–$5 for estate varietal wine.

TOURS: Public tours available three times a day. Private tours by appointment.

THE WINES: Blanc de Noirs, Chardonnay, Merlot, Pinot Noir, Sonoma Brut.

SPECIALTIES: Brut Rosé, Carneros Cuvée, Extra Brut, Gravel Knob Vineyard Pinot Noir, José S. Ferrer Reserve, Royal Cuvée, Rust Rock Terrace Pinot Noir, Va de Vi sparkling wine.

WINEMAKERS: Bob Iantosca and Steven Urberg.

ANNUAL PRODUCTION: 150,000 cases.

OF SPECIAL NOTE: Spanish cookbooks and locally made products, as well as deli items, sold at the winery. Annual Catalan Festival (July).

NEARBY ATTRACTIONS: Mission San Francisco Solano and other historic buildings in downtown Sonoma; Sonoma Raceway (NASCAR and other events); biplane flights; Cornerstone Sonoma (garden installations and tours).

D. H. Gustafson Family Vineyard

D. H. Gustafson Family Vineyard
9100 Skaggs Springs Rd.
Geyserville, CA 95441
707-433-2371
info@gfvineyard.com
www.gfvineyard.com

Owners: Dan, Kristen, and Jeff Gustafson.

Location: 17 miles northwest of Healdsburg.

Appellation: Dry Creek Valley.

Hours: Saturday, 10 A.M.– 4 P.M., or by appointment.

Tastings: Complimentary.

Tours: Guided tours of winery and vineyard ($25), including tasting, by reservation.

The Wines: Estate-grown Cabernet Sauvignon, Petite Sirah, Riesling, Rosé of Syrah, Sauvignon Blanc, Syrah, Zinfandel.

Specialties: Petite Sirah, Late Harvest Red (Port-style dessert wine), Zinfandel.

Winemaker: Emmett Reed; consulting winemaker: Kerry Damskey.

Annual Production: 4,000 cases.

Of Special Note: A 300-year-old, 11-foot-diameter madrone on property is believed to be the largest madrone in Sonoma County. Picnic area with panoramic views.

Nearby Attraction: Lake Sonoma (swimming, fishing, boating, camping, hiking).

On a quiet country road winding through the foothills above Dry Creek Valley, D. H. Gustafson Family Vineyard sits at a lofty 1,800 feet above sea level. Seemingly remote, yet less than thirty minutes from Healdsburg, this crowd-free getaway offers intimate wine tastings and a tranquil spot for a picnic. Ancient madrones and oaks blanket the 247-acre property with a year-round canopy of green. From the winery, panoramic views include Napa County, thirty miles to the east, and Mount St. Helena. At the rustic hilltop picnic area, visitors can see the Mayacamas Range in the distance and shimmering Lake Sonoma.

With twenty acres of vineyards ranging in elevation from 1,600 to 1,800 feet, the former sheep ranch is one of the highest elevation wineries in Sonoma County. Owner Dan Gustafson, a Minnesota farm boy who became a prominent real estate developer and landscape architect, purchased the property in 2002 and planted his vineyards with an eye to preserving the natural features, while leaving the rest of the property as an ecological preserve. Local lore relates that where madrones grow well, so will grapes, and the region's red volcanic soil provides the quick drainage grapes prefer and the lean, dry conditions that produce small berries with concentrated flavors.

Farming practices are strictly sustainable and include the use of blando brome, an annual grass, and red clover as cover crops to replenish the soil. The vineyards grow within a ten-minute walk of the winery, allowing winemaker Emmett Reed to inspect the rows daily. Consulting winemaker Kerry Damskey, noted for making stylish red wines from high-elevation vineyards, works closely with Reed, who lives on the property and oversees the vineyard and the winemaking process. Together, they create memorable wines—made entirely from handpicked estate fruit—ranging from crisp Riesling to bold Zinfandel.

The stunning house was designed by architect Tim Bjella to wed visually with the site. The red stone foundation matches the color of the soil, and the curves and angles of the roofline mirror the rolling hills in the valley below. The square tower rising dramatically from the center of the residence appears in a stylized version on the winery's label. The intimate tasting room is often staffed by owner Dan Gustafson, winemaker Emmett Reed, or tasting room manager Kaitlin Reed. The space has a concrete bar, tall black leather chairs, and display shelves built from reclaimed wood. In this inviting room, midwestern hospitality prevails amid the mountain air and rural hush of Sonoma County's high country.

JCB BY JEAN-CHARLES BOISSET

ine, art, and style from France and California unite at JCB's chic tasting room in Healdsburg. Old-World elements—a crystal chandelier, an antique champagne saber—transport visitors to an ambience more like Paris than rural Sonoma County. The JCB Collection of wines, created by wine entrepreneur Jean-Charles Boisset, celebrates the synergy of traditions from his native France and avant-garde approaches to winemaking in California, his adopted home. Boisset grew up in a winemaking family in Burgundy. Today, he, along with his parents and sister, owns more than twenty wine estates in Burgundy and California.

When Boisset started JCB in 2006, he wanted to create a collection that expressed his personal, lifelong connections to winemaking. He also wanted to offer a more interactive wine-tasting experience in which each sip triggers a vivid memory or emotional response. Each year, Boisset and his team of winemakers walk the cellars at the family's wineries in California and Burgundy, tasting from every barrel and choosing only those stylish enough to become JCB wines. They then decide which of these select barrels to blend with others. This stylistic approach takes winemaking beyond the influences from a single vineyard or *terroir*. For Boisset, each wine is like an artistic composition with an individual style.

Each JCB wine bears a number that symbolizes significant experiences in Boisset's life. A series of three adjectives also describes each wine's style—for example, *audacious, passionate, mysterious*—which are characteristics that Boisset attempts to replicate with each vintage. The N° 3 Pinot Noir, first released in 2012, is among the first Franco-American wine blends ever made. It refers to a sum that is greater than its parts (one plus one equals three) and celebrates the birth of Boisset's twin daughters. The N° 7 Pinot Noir reflects Boisset's age when he snuck a few tastes of Grand Cru wines that his parents were serving at a dinner party. The N° 81 Chardonnay recalls the excitement Boisset felt in 1981, when as a boy he first toured California wine country.

Guests in the luxurious JCB tasting room on Healdsburg Plaza can enjoy wines by the glass or traditional tasting flights of current releases in the JCB Collection. On the wall, side-by-side chalkboard drawings of Côte d'Or, Burgundy, France, and Sonoma County appellation maps summarize the JCB philosophy: "Oceans of the world separate us, wines of the world unite us."

JCB BY JEAN-CHARLES BOISSET
320 Center St.
Healdsburg, CA 95448
707-473-9707
tastingroom@jcbwines.com
www.jcbwines.com

OWNER: Boisset Family Estates.

LOCATION: Corner of Center St. and Plaza St. on Healdsburg Plaza.

APPELLATIONS: Burgundy, Mendocino, Napa Valley, Russian River Valley, Sonoma Coast.

HOURS: 11 A.M.–7 P.M. Thursday–Saturday; 11 A.M.–5:30 P.M. Sunday–Monday; Tuesday–Wednesday by appointment.

TASTINGS: $18 for 5 wines; reservations recommended.

TOURS: None.

THE WINES: Brut Burgundy, Brut Burgundy Rosé, Cabernet Franc, Cabernet Sauvignon, Chardonnay, Pinot Noir.

SPECIALTIES: Limited-production wines from Burgundy and California.

WINEMAKER: Jean-Charles Boisset.

ANNUAL PRODUCTION: 5,000 cases.

OF SPECIAL NOTE: Baccarat crystal and other merchandise sold in tasting room. Collection of numbered-edition wines available only in tasting room.

NEARBY ATTRACTIONS: Riverfront Regional Park (hiking, fishing, boating, wildlife viewing); Russian River (swimming, canoeing, kayaking, rafting, fishing); Healdsburg Museum and Historical Society; Hand Fan Museum (collection of antique fans).

Jordan Vineyard & Winery

Jordan Vineyard & Winery
1474 Alexander Valley Rd.
Healdsburg, CA 95448
707-431-5250
800-654-1213
info@jordanwinery.com
www.jordanwinery.com

Owner: John Jordan.

Location: About 4 miles
northeast of Healdsburg.

Appellation:
Alexander Valley.

Hours: 8 A.M.–4:30 P.M.
Monday–Friday; 9 A.M.–
3:30 P.M. Saturday. Open
Sundays May–October.

Tastings: By appointment.

Tours: By appointment.

The Wines: Cabernet
Sauvignon, Chardonnay.

Specialties: Alexander
Valley Cabernet
Sauvignon, Russian
River Valley Chardonnay.

Winemaker: Rob Davis.

Annual Production:
90,000 cases.

Of Special Note: Extensive
landscaped grounds and
gardens, including Tuscan
olive trees. Jordan estate
extra-virgin olive oil
sold at winery. Library
and large-format wines
available only at winery.

Nearby Attractions:
Lake Sonoma (boating,
camping, hiking, fishing,
swimming); Jimtown
Store (country market,
homemade foods).

P arts of Sonoma County resemble the French wine country, but mostly in a topographical sense. The picture always lacked a key element: a grand château. That changed in 1972, when Tom Jordan established his estate in Alexander Valley. Inspired by several eighteenth-century châteaus in southwestern France, the winery, situated on an oak-studded knoll, was designed by the San Francisco architectural firm of Backen, Arrigoni & Ross. The château, with its classic wine-red doors and shutters, also serves as a visual metaphor for the winemaking philosophy at Jordan, where Cabernet Sauvignon and Chardonnay are crafted in the French tradition with the hallmarks of balance, elegance, and food affinity.

As visitors approach on the winding driveway, they are teased with glimpses of the château until they reach the top of the hill and can see the entire structure and its landscaped grounds. The image of an old-world French gardens with their clipped pollarded sycamores. Boston ivy changes colors with the seasons. bronze statue of Bacchus, a copy original in the National Museum every vantage affords panoramic its most dramatic focal points,

estate is furthered by the formal privet hedges, poplar trees, and clinging to the château walls Gracing the entrance is a small of Jacopo Sansovino Tatti's 1512 in Florence. From the hilltop, vistas of Alexander Valley and Geyser Peak and Mount St. Helena. It was ancient volcanic activity from Geyser Peak, along with eons of seismic uplift, that formed the narrow, twenty-mile-long valley named for the pioneering family who began farming this area in 1847.

By 1974 Tom Jordan had acquired more than 1,500 acres, which included two lakes and plenty of room for the château and winery facility. After an enlightening trip to Italy in 1995, he planted the first grove of Tuscan olive trees, whose fruit is pressed for the winery's award-winning estate extra-virgin olive oil. Then, in 2005, after taking the helm of the family winery, son John embarked on various initiatives to enhance the winemaking and sustainable farming practices while reducing the winery's carbon footprint.

The winery also elevated its hospitality experience for visitors. Each tour culminates with a tasting of current releases, a library wine, and a selection of seasonal bites and artisan cheeses in the comfortable cellar room. Guests are welcome to enjoy intimate seated tastings without the tour.

KELLER ESTATE

White rail fences frame the road to Keller Estate, an architectural gem set among the windswept pastures and wetlands bordering the Petaluma River. The 650-acre property rests in the Petaluma Gap, an up-and-coming part of the Sonoma Coast appellation, where breezes off San Pablo Bay can whip through at fifty miles per hour. The region receives ample sunshine, however, which prompted Deborah and Arturo Keller to plant thirteen acres of Chardonnay in 1989.

By 2000 the Kellers, with help from Arturo's daughter, Ana, had begun transforming the appellation's southernmost winery into a superior wine estate. They expanded their thirteen-acre vineyard to ninety acres of Chardonnay Syrah, Viognier, and Pinot Ana ensured a diversity of fruit by planting vineyard blocks land around the blocks retains 2,000 olive trees planted for

and Pinot Noir, as well as some Gris. As director of the winery, for the all-estate-grown wine throughout the property. The its open-range look, save for making olive oil.

Built in 2003, the winery is an arresting low-profile structure of straight lines and gentle curves. It was designed by the late Ricardo Legoretta, an acclaimed Mexican architect famed for his playful use of light, color, and geometric forms. Covering the exterior are quarried stones—some bearing fossils and even tombstone engravings—salvaged from a Chinese village in advance of flooding for the Three Gorges Dam. From the flat roof rise a cylinder and volcano-like cone that funnel sunshine into the cellar. Inside, these skylights glow like giant yellow polka dots, as decorative as they are functional.

Originally from Mexico, Arturo Keller is a retired automotive manufacturer and avid collector of vintage automobiles. Antique cars drew him to the Petaluma area, where he found a hub of fellow aficionados.

The atmosphere at Keller is relaxed and engaging as tasters admire southerly views of the Petaluma Gap and 2,571-foot Mount Tamalpais in Marin County. San Francisco lies at the horizon, about thirty-five miles away. Once part of the ancient seabed of San Pablo Bay, the region's diverse soils lend a unified thread of lively minerality to the wines. Seated tastings are poured on a broad patio with teak furniture grouped under wisteria laden arbors. The tasting room is a Spanish Colonial blend of warm-hued wood and local stone. Doors at the back open into a four-hundred-foot-long, cement-walled cave holding more than two hundred oak barrels. Cellar workers have painted bands of crimson stain on the barrels reserved for red wine, lending ribbons of jewel tones to the shadowy cave.

KELLER ESTATE
5875 Lakeville Hwy.
Petaluma, CA 94954
707-765-2117
www.kellerestate.com

OWNERS: Keller family.

LOCATION: 7 miles southeast of downtown Petaluma.

APPELLATION: Sonoma Coast.

HOURS: 11 A.M.–4 P.M. Friday–Sunday, by appointment (same-day appointments available).

TASTINGS: Sit-down tastings. $15 for 5 wines.

TOURS: Cave and barrel tour and tasting in reserve room ($40), 11:30 A.M. and 2 P.M., Friday and Saturday; reservations recommended. Signature Reserve Tour and Tasting ($75); reservation required.

THE WINES: Chardonnay, Pinot Gris, Pinot Noir, Syrah.

SPECIALTIES: Single-vineyard Chardonnay and Pinot Noir.

WINEMAKER: Alberto Rodriguez.

ANNUAL PRODUCTION: 5,000 cases.

OF SPECIAL NOTE: All wines and olive oil are estate grown. Vintage car from owner's collection on display. Winery is pet friendly.

NEARBY ATTRACTIONS: Shollenberger Park (hiking, bird-watching); San Pablo Bay National Wildlife Refuge (hiking, fishing, interpretive program); Sonoma Raceway (NASCAR and other events).

LEDSON WINERY & VINEYARDS

LEDSON WINERY & VINEYARDS
7335 Hwy. 12
Kenwood, CA 95409
707-537-3810
www.ledson.com

OWNER:
Steve Noble Ledson.

LOCATION: About 2 miles northwest of the town of Kenwood.

APPELLATION: Sonoma Valley.

HOURS: 10 A.M.–5 P.M. daily

TASTINGS: $15 for 6 wines; $20 for 9 wines; $25 for wine consultant picks; $35 for private tasting. Cheese trays available.

TOURS: Self-guided.

THE WINES: Barbera, Cabernet Franc, Cabernet Sauvignon, Carignane, Chardonnay, Grenache, Malbec, Meritage, Merlot, Mourvèdre, Orange Muscat, Petite Sirah, Petit Verdot, Pinot Noir, Port, Riesling, Sangiovese, Sauvignon Blanc, Syrah, Zinfandel.

SPECIALTIES: Small lots of handcrafted Cabernet Sauvignon, Chardonnay, Merlot, Sauvignon Blanc, Zinfandel.

WINEMAKER:
Steve Noble Ledson.

ANNUAL PRODUCTION:
35,000 cases.

OF SPECIAL NOTE:
Wines only available at winery, hotel, and online. Gourmet Marketplace offers a variety of foods. Ledson Hotel & Centre du Vin, a 6-room hotel, wine bar, and restaurant, located on Sonoma Plaza.

NEARBY ATTRACTION:
Annadel State Park (hiking, biking).

I t came to be known widely as "The Castle"—some people say it reminds them of a French castle in Normandy. The architectural showpiece took ten years and some two million bricks to build. When the Ledson family started construction in 1992, they thought the property would be ideal for their residence. They planted Merlot vineyards and began work on the house. As the months passed, the turrets, slate roofs, balconies, and fountains took shape, and passersby would even climb over the fence to get a better look.

Steve Ledson finally realized it was time to rethink his plan. Given the intense public interest in the building and the quality of the grape harvests—which were sold to nearby wineries—he decided to turn the 16,000-square-foot structure into a winery and tasting room. In 1997 he released the winery's first wine: the 1994 Estate Merlot. After two years of reconstruction, the winery opened in 1999.

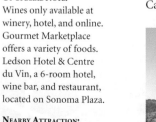

Fortunately, Ledson not only had his own construction company but also benefited from his family's history of farming in the area, beginning in the 1860s. His great-great-grandfather on his father's side was an early pioneer in Sonoma County winemaking, and both sets of grandparents had worked adjoining Sonoma Valley ranches cooperatively. Eventually, this Ledson acreage became part of the Annadel State Park. The family had grown grapes for years, so Steve, the fifth generation to farm in the area, jumped at the chance to buy the twenty-one-acre property to plant Estate Merlot. The winery produces more than eighty different wines, with a wide range of varietals and a broad spectrum of price levels.

Visitors to The Castle find an estate worthy of the French countryside, with a grand brick driveway, a manicured landscape, and a flourishing collection of roses. Just inside the front door is a grand staircase that reminds people of the movie *Gone with the Wind*. The Castle has more than five miles of ceiling moldings and 16,000 square feet of hardwood flooring spread over four floors of twenty-seven rooms, each with a different pattern of wood inlays. Twelve rooms are visible to the public: nine tasting rooms, a gourmet marketplace, a parlor area, and a club room.

At Ledson, visitors are treated to a sensory feast. The Gourmet Marketplace features a tempting selection of gourmet meats, artisan cheeses, fresh made-to-order sandwiches, salads, and desserts, as well as an extensive selection of locally produced gourmet items, including olive oils. Guests can enjoy a picnic lunch outdoors at tables overlooking the estate vineyards and fountains, or in The Castle's intimate parlor with its elegant Italian marble fireplaces and breathtaking views.

MERRIAM VINEYARDS

When Peter and Diana Merriam wed in 1982, they honeymooned among the vineyards of France. The trip ignited a passion for wine, and in 1988 the New England natives bought a wine shop near Boston. They frequently traveled to France on business and to immerse themselves in the country's culture of food and wine. Eager to start a winery and promote that culture at home, the couple began searching for vineyard property in 1995. They understood that quality grapes are required to produce fine wine and hoped to buy an established vineyard boasting pedigreed fruit. They sought advice from an old friend from Maine, Tom Simoneau, a winemaker and radio personality who had moved to Sonoma County and planted his own vineyard in 1988. With his help, they found the eleven-acre Windacre Vineyard, near Healdsburg. In 2000 the couple purchased the property, which had originally been planted to wine grapes in 1890. Located in the warmest corner of the Russian River Valley appellation, the vineyard was replanted in 2003 with Bordeaux varieties.

The Merriams blended their first vintage of California-style Bordeaux in 2000, three years before finding ideal acreage for the winery on the east side of the Russian River. It took six years to secure permits and finish construction, and in 2009 the winery and tasting room opened. That same year, the couple planted a second estate vineyard to Pinot Noir, Sauvignon Blanc, and Semillon on eight acres surrounding the winery. The vineyard was certified organic in 2011. The winery supplements estate fruit by purchasing Cabernet Sauvignon from Gloeckner-Smith in the Rockpile AVA, Cabernet Franc from Jones Vineyard in Dry Creek Valley, and Chardonnay from Simoneau and Bacigalupi Vineyards.

The winery and tasting room stand on a low hill with views of rolling vineyards and coastal ridges to the west. Steeply pitched roofs and wide covered porches give the structures a New England flavor. Inside, the tasting room resembles a spacious farmhouse, complete with hand-hewn oak floors and an old table with a traditional soapstone top. Antique furnishings include a bottle corker, a carpenter's bench, and harvest baskets, as well as a polished wooden bench that serves as a window seat.

Several of the wines are served with small bites prepared on-site. Pairings include crostini with artisanal cheese, pâté, and chocolate, depending on the wine poured. The Merriams, who divide their time between New England and Sonoma County, sell 60 percent of their wine to restaurants and retailers back east, reserving most of the other 40 percent for the tasting room.

MERRIAM VINEYARDS
11650 Los Amigos Rd.
Healdsburg, CA 95448
707-433-4032
tastingroom@
merriamvineyards.com
www.merriamvineyards.
com

OWNERS: Peter and Diana
Merriam.

LOCATION: 3.5 miles south
of Healdsburg.

APPELLATION: Russian River
Valley.

HOURS: 10 A.M.–5 P.M. daily.

TASTINGS: $5 for Signature
wines. $10 for reserve
wines includes small bite
pairings. Fee refunded
with wine purchase. $20
for 8 wines paired with
bites and 4 different
cheeses, by appointment.

TOURS: Complimentary
tours by appointment
made 24 hours in advance.

THE WINES: Cabernet
Franc, Cabernet
Sauvignon, Chardonnay,
Merlot, Petit Verdot, Pinot
Noir, Sauvignon Blanc.

SPECIALTIES: Estate Pinot
Noir, red Bordeaux blends,
Miktos (red Bordeaux
blend).

WINEMAKER:
David Herzberg.

ANNUAL PRODUCTION:
2,500 cases.

OF SPECIAL NOTE: Library
wines tasted on rotating
basis. Fine art and
photographs by local
artists for sale in tasting
room. New England
lobster bake held in
July, Harvest Dinner in
October.

NEARBY ATTRACTION:
Russian River (swimming,
canoeing, kayaking,
rafting, fishing).

PAPAPIETRO PERRY

PAPAPIETRO PERRY
4791 Dry Creek Rd.
Healdsburg, CA 95448
877-467-4668
707-433-0422
info@papapietro-perry.
com
www.papapietro-perry.
com

OWNERS: Bruce and Renae
Perry, Ben and Yolanda
Papapietro.

LOCATION: 4.7 miles
northwest of Healdsburg.

APPELLATIONS: Anderson
Valley, Dry Creek Valley,
Russian River Valley,
Sonoma Coast.

HOURS: 11 A.M.–4:30 P.M.
daily.

TASTINGS: $10 for 5 wines.

TOURS: None.

THE WINES: Chardonnay,
Pinot Noir, Zinfandel.

SPECIALTY: Pinot Noir.

WINEMAKER:
Ben Papapietro.

ANNUAL PRODUCTION:
6,000–8,000 cases.

OF SPECIAL NOTE: Covered
patio with tables and views
of Dry Creek Valley; picnic
area; bocce ball. Annual
events include Winter
Wineland (January),
Barrel Tasting (March),
Passport to Dry Creek
Valley (April), Chardonnay
and Lobster (June), and
Wine & Food Affair
(November).

NEARBY ATTRACTIONS:
Lake Sonoma (hiking,
fishing, boating, camping,
swimming); Russian River
(swimming, canoeing,
kayaking, rafting, fishing);
Healdsburg Museum and
Historical Society; Hand
Fan Museum (collection
of antique fans).

A passion for Pinot Noir has connected Ben Papapietro and Bruce Perry for nearly forty years. Both grew up in San Francisco, in Italian and Portuguese families who always served wine at meals and gatherings. Their grandfathers made wine at home in the basement, and the young boys watched and listened, learning the basic techniques of the craft. They also developed a keen, lifelong interest in cooking and wine.

As a young man, Ben Papapietro sampled various Burgundian wines and fell in love with Pinot Noir. Purchasing this varietal for daily consumption, however, would certainly break the family bank. So he began making his own wines at home in the garage, following his ancestral traditions. In the 1970s while working at the San Francisco Newspaper Agency, he became friends with another avid home winemaker, Burt Williams. In the early 1980s, Williams cofounded Williams Selyem, a Sonoma winery famed for its Pinot Noir production. Papapietro volunteered there during annual harvests for more than a decade and was able to learn and hone his own skills at winemaking.

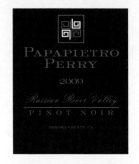

A few years later Bruce Perry, who also worked at the San Francisco Newspaper Agency, sampled Ben Papapietro's garage-made wines and joined in on the endeavor. After trying several varietals, it was Pinot Noir that won their hearts. More than a decade later, the friends felt ready to introduce their Pinot Noir to the public. They located a winemaking facility in Sonoma County and founded Papapietro Perry Winery in 1998. They eventually left their day jobs and dove full force into the business, with Bruce and Ben making the wine and Bruce's wife, Renae, running the business. Later, Ben's wife, Yolanda, joined to handle distributor relations.

The devoted attention paid off quickly, as Papapietro Perry wines have consistently earned high praise and awards from critics since the early 2000s. Ben Papapietro's winemaking skills have also garnered acclaim among Pinot Noir devotees. Today the winery produces ten Pinot Noirs, two Zinfandels, and a tiny amount of Chardonnay. Grapes come from established vineyards in the Russian River Valley, as well as surrounding Dry Creek Valley, Anderson Valley, and the Sonoma Coast.

The Papapietro Perry tasting room opened in 2005 at Timber Crest Farms, in the heart of pastoral Dry Creek Valley. The former farm now houses a collection of wineries and other small businesses. Visitors taste wines at a gleaming copper-topped bar made of intricately woven barrel staves, which Bruce Perry built by hand. In many ways, the unpretentious space reflects the winery's homey, but humble beginnings in the family garage more than three decades past.

RAMEY WINE CELLARS

S ome winemakers plan, plot, and scheme for years, if not decades, before they can establish their own winery. In David Ramey's case, the process was decidedly more casual, even spur-of-the-moment. Not that he didn't have decades of experience before he founded Ramey Wine Cellars in 1996. Ramey had long been acknowledged as one of the pioneers who challenged the status quo among American winemakers and helped propel California into the spotlight on the international wine stage. From the start, Ramey has spent his entire career in the big leagues.

After a traditional beginning—a graduate degree from the University of California at Davis—Ramey struck out for France  for a stint at Château Pétrus in Pomerol, a small but distinctive wine region in Bordeaux known for producing opulent red wines. He returned to California the following year, French winemaking lessons learned, and was hired by Simi Winery in Healdsburg as assistant winemaker to Zelma Long. In 1984 he replaced Merry Edwards as winemaker at Matanzas Creek and then spent six years at Chalk Hill Estate. During the 1990s, he also worked with Leslie Rudd, of Rudd Estate, and spent two years making Bordeaux-style wines at Dominus Estate, owned by Christian Moueix, of Pétrus.

It was at Dominus that Ramey had his "aha!" moment. Dominus made only red wines, but Ramey wanted to make whites as well. When Moueix told him he was welcome "to make a little Chardonnay on the side," Ramey seized the opportunity. Along with his wife, Carla, he produced his first wine under the Ramey Wine Cellars label, 260 cases of Chardonnay sourced from the prestigious Hyde Vineyard in the Carneros appellation. It would be another five years before Ramey had a winemaking facility of his own. Still, it was hardly what could be called a grand plan: instead of creating a fancy estate, he set up shop in 2003 in a metal building located in a largely residential neighborhood in the heart of Healdsburg. Four years later, having outgrown the original space, Ramey opened a new winery a few blocks away in an industrial park. The original winery is used mostly for red wines; the new facility, for whites.

The new site is unadorned, aside from the entrance, which is landscaped with soaring palms, Japanese maples, and a smattering of native plants. Visitors are welcome to look around, but there are no tours per se. Tastings are conducted in a second-floor room, where sixteen people can be seated at a time, with nothing to distract them from focusing on the wines that Ramey handcrafts by fusing old-world traditions, California *terroir*, and New World innovations.

RAMEY WINE CELLARS
25 Healdsburg Ave.
Healdsburg, CA 95448
707-433-0870 ext. 2102
info@rameywine.com
www.rameywine.com

OWNERS: David and Carla Ramey.

LOCATION: .5 mile south of Healdsburg Plaza.

APPELLATIONS: Napa, including Los Carneros and Oakville; Sonoma, including Russian River Valley and Sonoma Coast.

HOURS: 10 A.M. and 2 P.M. Monday–Saturday, by appointment.

TASTINGS: $25 for 6–10 current releases.

TOURS: None.

THE WINES: Cabernet Sauvignon, Chardonnay, Syrah.

SPECIALTIES: Single-vineyard and single-appellation Cabernet Sauvignon, Chardonnay, Syrah.

WINEMAKER: David Ramey.

ANNUAL PRODUCTION: 30,000 cases.

OF SPECIAL NOTE: Leisurely, sit-down tastings last at least an hour. Library wines and large-format wines available only in the tasting room.

NEARBY ATTRACTIONS: Riverfront Regional Park (hiking, fishing, boating, wildlife viewing); Russian River (swimming, canoeing, kayaking, rafting, fishing); Healdsburg Museum and Historical Society; Hand Fan Museum (collection of antique fans).

RAVENSWOOD WINERY

RAVENSWOOD WINERY
18701 Gehricke Rd.
Sonoma, CA 95476
707-938-1960
888-669-4679
www.ravenswoodwinery.
com

OWNER:
Constellation Brands.

LOCATION: About .5 mile
northeast of the town of
Sonoma via Fourth St.
East and Lovall Valley Rd.

APPELLATION:
Sonoma Valley.

HOURS: 10 A.M.–4:30 P.M.
daily.

TASTINGS: $10 for county
series; $15 for vineyard-
designated wines.

TOURS: 10:30 A.M. daily.

THE WINES: Bordeaux-style
blends, Cabernet Franc,
Cabernet Sauvignon,
Chardonnay, Icon (blend
of Zinfandel, Carignane,
Petite Sirah, and Alicante
Bouschet), Muscato, Petite
Sirah, Zinfandel.

SPECIALTY: Zinfandel.

WINEMAKER: Joel Peterson.

ANNUAL PRODUCTION:
500,000 cases.

OF SPECIAL NOTE: Blending
seminars by appointment.
Bicyclists and other
visitors are welcome to
picnic on stone patio with
view of vineyards.

NEARBY ATTRACTIONS:
Mission San Francisco
Solano and other historic
buildings in downtown
Sonoma; bike rentals; Vella
Cheese Company; Sonoma
Cheese Factory; Sonoma
Traintown (rides on a scale
railroad).

Few wineries set out to make cult wines, and probably fewer earn a widespread following as well. Ravenswood has done both. Its founders began by crushing enough juice to produce 327 cases of Zinfandel in 1976, and although the winery also makes other wines, Zinfandel remains king. Nearly three-quarters of Ravenswood's production is Zinfandel.

Winemaker and cofounder Joel Peterson and chairman and cofounder Reed Foster were so successful with that first, handcrafted vintage that they have had to live up to the standard it set ever since. Ravenswood produces fourteen different Zinfandels that repre- sent the spectrum of the varietal's personality, with tastes ranging from peppery and spicy to chocolaty and minty. If there is one common denominator, it is reflected in the slogan adopted by the winery in 1990: "No Wimpy Wines."

Most of Ravenswood's grapes come from more than a hundred independent growers. It is those long-standing relationships that ensure the consistency of the wines. One vineyard source dates to 1986.

The Strotz family invited Joel Peterson to visit their Sonoma Mountain vineyard, which they had named Pickberry because of all the wild blackberries harvested there. Peterson immediately recognized the quality of the Strotz grapes, and in 1988 Ravenswood released the first of its many blends of Cabernet Sauvignon, Cabernet Franc, and Merlot under the vineyard-designated name Pickberry.

Peterson never set out to specialize in Zinfandel; originally he was more interested in the Bordeaux varietals he began tasting at the age of ten with his father, Walter, founder of the San Francisco Wine Sampling Club. In time, however, he fell under the spell of Zinfandel. In the 1970s, after a brief career as a wine writer and consultant, he went to work for the late Joseph Swan, considered one of California's outstanding craftsmen of fine Zinfandel. Thus the stage was set for the varietal's ascendancy at the winery Peterson founded.

Ravenswood farms fourteen acres of estate vineyards on the northeast side of Sonoma. The old stone building, once home to the Haywood Winery, has extensive patio seating with beautiful south-facing views of the vineyards. Thanks to the company's growth, the winemaking operations have since been relocated to a 45,000-square-foot facility in Carneros, to the south, but the tasting room remains. Originally a cozy, even cramped affair, it was greatly expanded in 1996, and now has plenty of elbow room as well as ample natural light for visitors who come to sample and appreciate the wines.

TASTING ROOM
OPEN FROM 10-4:30

NO
BUSSES
PLEASE

PARKING

SBRAGIA FAMILY VINEYARDS

Just before Dry Creek Road reaches its western terminus at Lake Sonoma, the Sbragia Family Vineyards winery, perched on a hill, comes into view. Visitors approach the winery on a winding driveway that passes through Zinfandel vineyards and lush gardens. Among the features they first see is the generous terrace overlooking the vineyards. The setting is an ideal one for an afternoon of tasting and enjoying the vista from the top of Dry Creek Valley, an impressive panorama that takes in Mount St. Helena on the eastern horizon.

Sbragia Family Vineyards is Ed Sbragia gained acclaim during winning wines at Beringer Vine- in 2008. Seven years before he left wine under the Sbragia Family winery's name, the business is a duties with his son, Adam. Adam's many miles from the place where his thirty years of making award-yards in Napa Valley before retiring Beringer, he had started producing Vineyards label. As reflected in the family affair. Ed Sbragia shares cellar wife, Kathy, is in charge of hospi-tality for the winery, and Ed's wife, Jane, and daughter, Gina, are often found behind the tasting bar.

The family's roots grow deepest in this part of Sonoma County. After purchasing land in Dry Creek Valley, the Sbragias grew and dried plums there for years. By the early 1960s, Ed's father, Gino Sbragia, had planted grapevines, which Ed helped tend until he went off to study chemistry at the University of California, Davis, and then earn an enology degree at Fresno State. Gino Sbragia, who died in 1995, had tried to start a winery, but Prohibition and the Great Depression prevented him from realizing his dream. Ed Sbragia promised his father that he would eventually establish a winery of his own. Among other endeavors, the family had run a restaurant and bar called the Ark. That name is honored today as a private reserve tasting room at the winery.

Ed and Adam Sbragia's focus is on making vineyard-designated wines. Five—Chardonnay, Sauvignon Blanc, Merlot, and two Zinfandels—are grown on estate vineyards. A vineyard owned by Ed's uncle provides fruit for another Zinfandel, and Chardonnay is also sourced from one of Ed's favorite vineyards, Gamble Ranch in Napa Valley. Fruit for five Sbragia Cabernet Sauvignons comes from various mountaintop vineyards: Andolsen Vineyard in Dry Creek Valley, Monte Rosso Vineyards in Sonoma's Mayacamas Range, Wall Vineyard on Mount Veeder in Napa, and Rancho Del Oso and Cimarossa Vineyard on Napa's Howell Mountain. Of the estate vineyards, two are named in honor of Gino Sbragia. Gino's Vineyard was planted to Zinfandel more than two decades ago. La Promessa Vineyard, also producing Zinfandel, acknowledges Ed's fulfilled promise to his father.

SBRAGIA FAMILY VINEYARDS
9990 Dry Creek Rd.
Geyserville, CA 95441
707-473-2992
info@sbragia.com
www.sbragia.com

OWNERS: Ed Sbragia and Jane Sbragia.

LOCATION: 10 miles northwest of Healdsburg.

APPELLATION: Dry Creek Valley.

HOURS: 11 A.M.–5 P.M. daily.

TASTINGS: $10–$20 for various tastings, including Dry Creek Valley, reserve Cabernet, and wine and cheese.

TOURS: By appointment only ($20).

THE WINES: Cabernet Sauvignon, Chardonnay, Merlot, Sauvignon Blanc, Zinfandel.

SPECIALTIES: Cabernet Sauvignon, Chardonnay, Zinfandel.

WINEMAKERS: Ed Sbragia, Adam Sbragia.

ANNUAL PRODUCTION: 12,500 cases.

OF SPECIAL NOTE: Winery specializes in single-vineyard wines. Tables and chairs for picnicking on an expansive terrace with views of the Dry Creek Valley. Prepared foods sold at winery. Annual events include Winter Wonderland (January), Barrel Tasting (March), and Passport Weekend (April).

NEARBY ATTRACTION: Lake Sonoma (swimming, fishing, boating, camping, hiking).

SCHUG CARNEROS ESTATE WINERY

SCHUG CARNEROS ESTATE WINERY
602 Bonneau Rd.
Sonoma, CA 95476
707-939-9363
800-966-9365
schug@schugwinery.com
www.schugwinery.com

OWNERS: Schug family.

LOCATION: .5 mile west of intersection of Hwy. 121 and Hwy. 12.

APPELLATION: Los Carneros.

HOURS: 10 A.M.–5 P.M. daily.

TASTINGS: $5 (applicable to wine purchase); $10 for reserve tasting (applicable to reserve wine purchase).

TOURS: By appointment.

THE WINES: Cabernet Sauvignon, Chardonnay, Merlot, Pinot Noir, Sauvignon Blanc, Sparkling Pinot Noir.

SPECIALTY: Pinot Noir.

WINEMAKER: Michael Cox.

ANNUAL PRODUCTION: 30,000 cases.

OF SPECIAL NOTE: Open house in late April and in mid-November (Holiday in Carneros). Courtyard tasting in summer.

NEARBY ATTRACTIONS: Mission San Francisco Solano and other historic buildings in downtown Sonoma; Sonoma Raceway (NASCAR and other events); biplane flights; Cornerstone Sonoma (innovative designs by landscape architects).

Fog and wind from the Pacific Ocean and San Francisco Bay sweep along the low, rocky hills of the Carneros appellation, where the volcanic soil, laden with clay, is shallow and dense. Grape growers intent on producing Cabernet Sauvignon and many other premium varietals avoid these conditions at all costs. But Walter Schug wanted to grow Pinot Noir, and he knew that this challenging combination of climate and geology would bring out the best in his favorite grape.

Walter Schug first made his reputation in the 1970s as the acclaimed winemaker for Joseph Phelps. Working at the ultrapremium Napa Valley winery, he was successful with a range of wine grapes, notably Cabernet Sauvignon, before turning his attention to Pinot Noir. In 1980, with grapes from a vineyard he had used at Phelps, Schug launched his own brand.

Schug and his wife, Gertrud, selected a fifty-acre site in the southern Sonoma Valley for their new vineyard estate and crowned the hilltop with a winery in 1990. They favored post-and-beam architecture reminiscent of Germany's Rhine River Valley, where the Schug family had long produced Pinot Noir. The style makes it one of the most instantly recognizable wineries in the appellation. Pinot Noir and Chardonnay vineyards surround the winery, and Schug has long-term contracts with other growers in Carneros to ensure the best grapes year after year. Protecting and enhancing the varietal and regional characteristics of the fruit are the essence of the Schug family's philosophy.

The European aspect of the Schug estate was enhanced with the excavation of an underground cave system in the mid-1990s. The system's naturally stable temperatures and humidity levels allow the wines to age gracefully in French oak barrels. Almost every inch of the caves is covered with gray concrete, but an exposed patch at the end of one tunnel affords a glimpse of the pockmarked, pumicelike volcanic rock characteristic of the region.

Visitors are warmly welcomed at this family-managed winery. From the hilltop tasting room, they are treated to spectacular views of the surrounding countryside. Nearby is a *pétanque* court, another nod to the Schugs' European ancestry. More than merely a sport, *pétanque* is a pastime that invites conviviality and conversation in the best old-world tradition.

ST. FRANCIS WINERY & VINEYARDS

I f St. Francis Winery & Vineyards wanted a catchy motto, it might be this: Come for the wine, stay for the food. The winery was one of the first in California to offer an extensive wine-and-food-pairing program and has never lost its leading edge. Executive chef Dave Bush creates seasonal menus of innovative dishes that complement the winery's many food-friendly varietals.

The culinary focus began shortly after St. Francis relocated one mile north of its modest origins to a new facility in 2001. Built in the style of the early California missions, the red-tile-roofed, sand-colored stucco hospitality

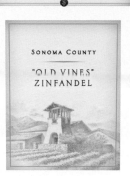

center is sited at the entrance of the venerable Wild Oak Vineyard, with Hood Mountain as a backdrop. A tower near the tasting room features a bell that is rung to mark every hour. The bell was cast by a historic Italian foundry and blessed in the Piazza della Basilica of St. Francis of Assisi.

Nearly thirty-five years ago, long before the wine world began to recognize the Sonoma County *terroir* as among the finest in the world, St. Francis Winery made the commitment to craft wines exclusively from Sonoma. With more than six hundred estate acres of prime vineyards in Sonoma Valley and Russian River Valley, St. Francis reaps the rewards of a bounty of outstanding fruit from superior mountain and valley vineyards in Sonoma County's best appellations.

The first stop for most visitors is the tasting room, where the beamed ceiling soars over twenty feet, and warmth is provided by wood paneling—and, in winter, by a roaring fireplace. Tasting is also on the patio, where umbrellas shade wooden tables and chairs arranged to create a spectacular vista of the lawns, gardens, and Hood Mountain. Inside and out, guests can enjoy flights of wine accompanied by chef-prepared charcuterie from 11 a.m. to 4 p.m. daily.

The Sonoma Valley's mild climate allows for being outdoors most of the year, especially from May through October. Throughout the year, multicourse wine-and-food pairings are available five days a week inside the winery's newly renovated dining room, with each session lasting about ninety minutes. Menus change seasonally to reflect the freshest products available locally, including vegetables from the winery's two-acre estate garden. The mouthwatering selections might include butter-poached salmon with Dungeness crab, paired with Sonoma County Chardonnay; duck confit flautas with mole, which brings out the fruit and spice in "Old Vines" Zinfandel; or a dessert course of chocolate fondue accompanied by port.

ST. FRANCIS WINERY & VINEYARDS
100 Pythian Rd.
(at Hwy. 12)
Santa Rosa, CA 95409
888-675-WINE (9463)
info@stfranciswinery.com
www.stfranciswinery.com

PRESIDENT AND CEO:
Christopher Silva.

LOCATION: Off Hwy. 12, 6 miles east of Santa Rosa and 1 mile west of Kenwood.

APPELLATION: Sonoma Valley.

HOURS: 10 A.M.–5 P.M. daily

TASTINGS: $10 for 5 wines; $25 for wine and charcuterie; $38 for multicourse food-and-wine pairing.

TOURS: Available only for groups of 10 or more with advance reservations.

THE WINES: Cabernet Franc, Cabernet Sauvignon, Chardonnay, Claret, Malbec, Merlot, Mourvèdre, Petite Sirah, Port, Sauvignon Blanc, Syrah, Viognier, Zinfandel.

SPECIALTIES: Wines from 100 percent handpicked Sonoma County grapes.

WINEMAKERS: Katie Madigan and Heather Munden.

ANNUAL PRODUCTION: 250,000 cases.

OF SPECIAL NOTE: Extensive wine-and-food pairings. Annual winery dinners and other events listed online, along with information on summer outdoor movie series.

NEARBY ATTRACTIONS: Sugarloaf Ridge State Park (hiking, camping, horseback riding); Annadel State Park (hiking, biking).

TALTY VINEYARDS & WINERY

TALTY VINEYARDS & WINERY
7127 Dry Creek Rd.
Healdsburg, CA 95448
707-433-8438
mtalty@taltyvineyards.com
www.taltyvineyards.com

OWNER: Michael Talty.

LOCATION: 7 miles
northwest of downtown
Healdsburg via Dry
Creek Rd.

APPELLATION: Dry Creek
Valley.

HOURS: 12 P.M.–4 P.M.
Friday–Monday. Tuesday–
Thursday by appointment.

TASTINGS: $10 for
4–6 wines.

TOURS: With winemaker/
owner Michael Talty, by
appointment.

THE WINE: Zinfandel.

SPECIALTY: Single-vineyard
Zinfandels.

WINEMAKER: Michael Talty.

ANNUAL PRODUCTION:
1,400–1,500 cases.

OF SPECIAL NOTE:
Winemaker usually pours
for guests. Events include
Barrel Tasting Weekend
(March) and Passport
Weekend (April). Wines
available only in tasting
room.

NEARBY ATTRACTION:
Lake Sonoma (hiking,
fishing, boating, camping,
swimming).

In the modern world of wine, it's unusual to find a winemaker who is involved in every step of the winemaking process. Michael Talty, proprietor of Talty Winery in the upper reaches of Dry Creek Valley, is one of these rare one-man shows. He prunes the vines, helps with harvest, and manages every stage from crush to bottle. Modest and unpretentious, Talty pours the wines in his tasting room and shares his deep passion for Zinfandel—the only grape varietal he uses in his craft. Talty's zeal and techniques have earned him acclaim as one of the best Zinfandel winemakers in Dry Creek Valley. In 2011 Talty Vineyards & Winery received the Winery of the Year award from Snooth.com. Many reviews highlight the characteristics that set Talty wines apart. They are typ- ically light, delicate, and elegant, which enables them to pair well with a range of foods. Most other Dry Creek Zinfan- dels pack a much more powerful, fruit-forward punch and pair best with robust dishes.

The winery's story begins with Michael Talty's father, William Talty, who loved to cook and enjoy fine wines—especially Zinfandels. The father-son duo planned for years to purchase a vineyard and establish a winery of their own. Sadly, William died suddenly in 1993, before their project came to fruition. Michael Talty and his family vowed to carry out William's dream. Michael studied enology at U.C. Davis and made wine in his San Jose garage. In 1997 the family bought a seven-acre parcel on the banks of Dry Creek and named it William Talty Estate in the patriarch's honor. Since the beginning, Michael Talty has personally performed all tasks involved in the winemaking process, starting in the dry-farmed, head-pruned estate vineyard, which includes fifty-year-old Zinfandel vines. He also sources fruit from two other vineyards, Filice Connolly Vineyard in Napa Valley and Dwight Family Vineyard in Dry Creek.

A visit to Talty Vineyards & Winery offers an exceptional opportunity to learn about wines firsthand from the expert himself in a down-to-earth setting. A long, paved driveway, lined with grapevines on one side and fruit trees on the other, leads to the farmhouse-style winery building next to the Taltys' home on the banks of Dry Creek. In a tiny tasting area filled with storage barrels, bottles, and framed images of awards and reviews, Michael Talty pours wines at marble-topped bar-rels, cheerfully sharing his knowledge and passion for Zinfandel. Bella, the Taltys' friendly winery dog, often greets visitors at the door. On the wall just inside the entrance hangs a striking photograph of William Talty, who in spirit is experiencing this joint venture with his son in the Zinfandel world.

VML WINERY

From downtown Healdsburg near Highway 101, Westside Road follows the western banks of the Russian River as it flows through verdant vineyards, orchards, and farmland toward the Pacific Ocean. VML Winery, named for winemaker Virginia Marie Lambrix, rests in the heart of this pastoral region, in an idyllic setting where the Earth's natural rhythms and human winemaking efforts flow in tandem. One of the newest wineries in the Russian River Valley, VML was established in 2011 on the site of the former Belvedere Winery. A team of partners owns the fifteen-acre certified organic vineyard and winemaking business: winemaker Virginia Marie Lambrix, Bill Hambrecht, brothers Paul and Heath Dolan, and Phil Hurst.

VML's tasting room and grounds are designed to inspire visitors to be responsible stewards of the planet. The setting stimulates the senses from the moment guests arrive. A shade garden with soaring redwood trees, a lily pond, picnic tables, and more than sixteen species of roses edge the parking area. Nearby, a stone stairway rises up to the redwood winery and tasting room. Exhibits of local art in the tasting room, including photography, paintings, and mixed media, rotate seasonally. The artwork on display is often for sale. Glass doors allow visitors to peek at the winemaking operations below.

Winemaker Lambrix often says she feels much like a sorceress in the vineyard, using a little "magic" to craft her wines. She sources most fruit from organic, mom-and-pop vineyards in the Russian River Valley, focusing on Pinot Noir and Chardonnay. She also makes Gewürztraminer, Rosé of Pinot Noir, Sauvignon Blanc, Syrah, Zinfandel, and sparkling wine. The VML label, derived from centuries-old drawings in alchemy, reflects Lambrix's contagious, fun-loving attitude and affinity for the magic of winemaking.

Lambrix's attitude extends to the patio and deck, where guests play Jenga with life-size pieces and listen to live music on Saturday afternoons. Gravel paths lead through a three-tiered garden that evokes the scents of Russian River Valley and provides a good way to develop the senses used in wine tasting. The highest terrace, Citrus Row, showcases eight varieties of citrus trees, plus olive trees. Down below are plants whose aromas and flavors are typically found in Russian River Valley Chardonnay (lemon verbena, apple, pear, basil, sage, almond) and Pinot Noir (raspberry, cherry, thyme, pomegranate, lavender, plum, rosemary). Hidden alcoves with benches create inviting "rooms" in which to relax and connect with the natural surroundings, as does the lowest tier—the shady redwood and rose oasis at the VML entrance.

VML WINERY
4035 Westside Rd.
Healdsburg, CA 95448
707-431-4404
info@vmlwine.com
www.vmlwine.com

OWNERS: Heath Dolan, Paul Dolan, Bill Hambrecht, Phil Hurst, Virginia Marie Lambrix.

LOCATION: 4 miles south of downtown Healdsburg.

APPELLATION: Russian River Valley.

HOURS: 11 A.M.–5 P.M. daily.

TASTINGS: $10 for 5–7 wines.

TOURS: Guided tours by appointment. Self-guided garden tour.

THE WINES: Chardonnay, Gewürztraminer, Pinot Noir, Rosé of Pinot Noir, Sauvignon Blanc, sparkling wine, Syrah, Zinfandel.

SPECIALTY: Russian River Valley single-vineyard Pinot Noir.

WINEMAKER: Virginia Marie Lambrix.

ANNUAL PRODUCTION: 7,000 cases.

OF SPECIAL NOTE: Spacious patio, deck, and gardens overlooking the Russian River Valley. Pet-friendly picnic area. Small selection of deli items for picnics. Food-and-wine pairings available by appointment. Tasting room showcases exhibits of local art. Annual events include Winter Wineland (January), Barrel Tasting (March), and Wine & Food Affair (November). Guest cottage available for rent.

NEARBY ATTRACTIONS: Russian River (swimming, canoeing, kayaking, rafting, fishing); Lake Sonoma (hiking, fishing, boating, camping, swimming).

MENDOCINO

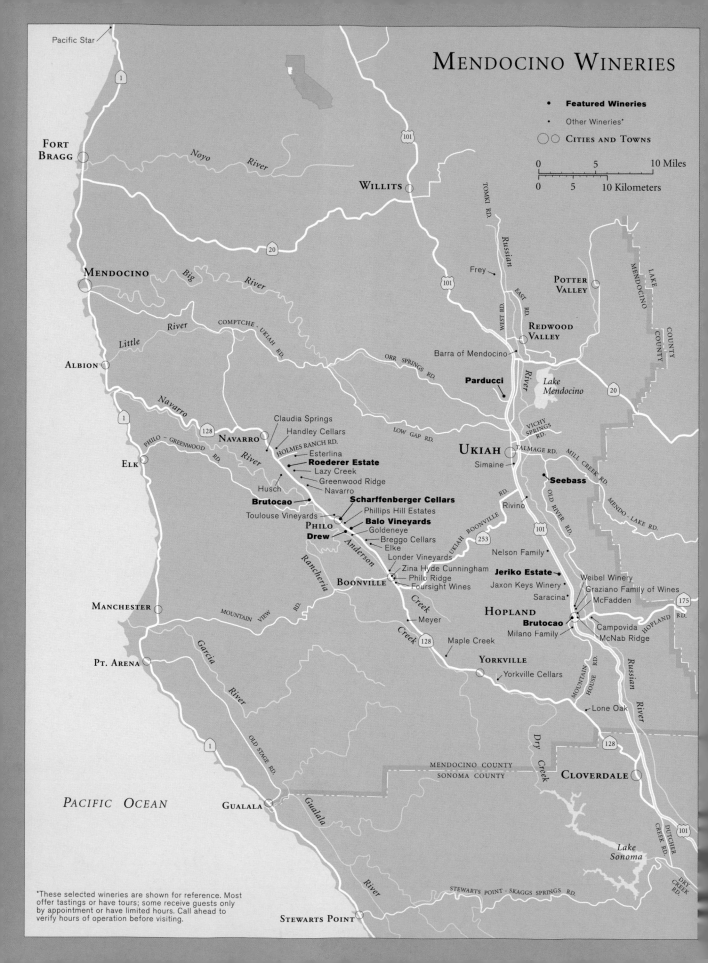

MENDOCINO WINERIES

● **Featured Wineries**
· Other Wineries*
◯ ◯ CITIES AND TOWNS

0   5   10 Miles

0   5   10 Kilometers

Pacific Star

1

FORT
BRAGG

Noyo River

WILLITS

101

TOMKI RD.

Russian

Frey

POTTER
VALLEY

20

101

EAST RD.

REDWOOD
VALLEY

MENDOCINO

Big River

Barra of Mendocino

LAKE MENDOCINO

COUNTY

River

COMPTCHE - UKIAH RD.

Little River

Lake
Mendocino

20

ALBION

ORR SPRINGS RD.

Parducci

River

Navarro

1

River

128

NAVARRO

LOW GAP RD.

VICHY SPRINGS RD.

PHILO - GREENWOOD RD.

Claudia Springs

Handley Cellars

HOLMES RANCH RD.

TALMAGE RD.

MILL CREEK RD.

ELK

Esterlina
Roederer Estate
Lazy Creek
Greenwood Ridge
Navarro

UKIAH

Simaine

Seebass

MENDO - LAKE RD.

Husch

River

Brutocao

Rivino

Toulouse Vineyards

Scharffenberger Cellars
Phillips Hill Estates
Balo Vineyards
Goldeneye
Breggo Cellars
Elke
Londer Vineyards
Zina Hyde Cunningham
Philo Ridge
Foursight Wines

PHILO
Drew

Anderson

RD.

UKIAH

BOONVILLE

253

101

OLD RIVER RD.

Nelson Family

Rancheria

BOONVILLE

Creek

Jeriko Estate
Jaxon Keys Winery
Saracina

Weibel Winery
Graziano Family of Wines
McFadden

175
RD.

MANCHESTER

MOUNTAIN VIEW RD.

Meyer

Creek

HOPLAND
Brutocao
Milano Family

Campovida
McNab Ridge

Creek

128

Maple Creek

PT. ARENA

Garcia

YORKVILLE

Yorkville Cellars

MOUNTAIN HOUSE RD.

HOPLAND RD.

Russian River

1

River

OLD STAGE RD.

Lone Oak

Dry Creek

128

MENDOCINO COUNTY

CLOVERDALE

SONOMA COUNTY

PACIFIC OCEAN

GUALALA

Gualala

River

Lake
Sonoma

101

DUTCHER CREEK RD.

DRY CREEK RD.

STEWARTS POINT - SKAGGS SPRINGS RD.

STEWARTS POINT

*These selected wineries are shown for reference. Most
offer tastings or have tours; some receive guests only
by appointment or have limited hours. Call ahead to
verify hours of operation before visiting.

Mendocino's dramatic coastline has made it famous all over the world, but the county offers a lot more than ocean views and rustic coastal inns. Now inland Mendocino is getting its due, thanks to local winemakers who are proving that their grapes are on a par with those of nearby Sonoma and Napa.

Vineyards were first planted here in the 1850s, when immigrants began farming food crops on the river plains and vineyards on the rugged hillsides and sun-exposed ridgetops. In time, they and their  successors found fertile ground in cooler areas that led them to achieve great success with a wide spec- trum of grape varieties.

Located too far north to transport their wines to the San Francisco market by boat—as Napa and Sonoma winemakers could—Mendocino's early grape growers sold and traded their crops closer to home. In the 1960s, the wine boom and advances in shipping brought Mendocino wines to markets farther afield. Today, the county boasts ninety-three wineries, so many of them involving organic wines or vineyards that the county bills itself as "America's Greenest Wine Region."

Mendocino's pioneer spirit still flourishes and is reflected in a serious respect for the environment. Most of the county is an undeveloped, pristine landscape offering abundant opportunities for enjoying an enviable variety of outdoor pursuits.

BALO VINEYARDS

A drive along scenic Highway 128 from the Mendocino coast or the inland Redwood Highway leads to picturesque Anderson Valley. Vineyards blanket many of the creekside meadows and mountain slopes. Hints of the region's history dot the landscape: sheep graze on verdant hillsides, and apple orchards edge many a vineyard. Balo Vineyards, on the site of a century-old sheep ranch, honors these Anderson Valley traditions. *Balo* means "to bleat" in Latin, and the winery label depicts a sheep and a grapevine, reminiscent of images in a medieval book on vellum (lambskin). Balo's stunning redwood tasting room and winery buildings rest at the edge of the hillside estate, just off the high-way in the quaint town of Philo. Tall, vented cupolas — the hallmark of the valley's historic apple dryer barns — rise from the rooftops, beckoning travelers to pull off the road for a casual wine country experience.

The Balo Vineyards story be-gan in North Carolina in the early 2000s with wine aficionados Tim and Michele Mullins and their children, Abigail and PJ. The family dreamed of moving to California to grow their own Pinot Noir. In 2003, after searching throughout the state for suitable property, they purchased an estate in the Anderson Valley with six acres of Pinot Noir vines planted in 1998. They quickly took steps to establish a premium, limited-production vineyard they could manage themselves. They planted additional Pinot Noir clones and in 2008 began farming organically. Later, they added two acres of Pinot Gris.

At first the family sold all their fruit to others. In 2009 they decided to begin their own wine-making venture. They retained some of their best estate fruit and called upon local winemaker Jason Drew to craft their inaugural vintage of 275 cases. Drew has served as winemaker ever since, while continuing to make wines for his own label. In the fall of 2012, Drew oversaw production of Balo Vineyards' first vintage made in the cutting-edge winery facility, completed earlier in the year.

The Balo Vineyards tasting room and grounds offer a laid-back setting for extended visits. Outdoors, visiting dogs run off energy in a shaded, enclosed area while guests play bocce ball on two competition-caliber courts or picnic on the terrace. Indoors, visitors taste wines at a black marble bar and relax by a stone fireplace, where a fire crackles on cool-weather days. An antique scale, which French negotiants once used to weigh wine barrels, stands in a corner amid furnishings made from recycled redwood. A vaulted ceiling displays an ever-growing collection of oil paintings created each year to promote annual Anderson Valley wine festivals — by local artist Gerald Reis, who also helped the family design a fitting winery label to honor the pastoral region.

BALO VINEYARDS
9001 Hwy. 128
Philo, CA 95466
707-895-3655
info@killerpinot.com
www.balovineyards.com

OWNERS: Michele and Tim Mullins.

LOCATION: 5 miles northwest of Boonville and 21 miles from Mendocino coast.

APPELLATION: Anderson Valley.

HOURS: 11 A.M.–5 P.M. Friday–Monday, and by appointment.

TASTINGS: Complimentary.

TOURS: Guided tours of winery, gardens, and vineyards on request.

THE WINES: Pinot Gris, Pinot Noir.

SPECIALTY: Small-lot estate wines using organically farmed grapes from mature vines.

WINEMAKER: Jason Drew.

ANNUAL PRODUCTION: 1,000–2,000 cases.

OF SPECIAL NOTE: Shaded, enclosed area for dogs. Two competition-caliber bocce courts. Picnic tables near bocce courts and on a stone terrace with performance stage. Small selection of local and regional deli items available for purchase. Annual events include International Alsace Varietals Festival (February) and Anderson Valley Pinot Noir Festival (May). Wines available for purchase by the glass. Most wines sold only in tasting room.

NEARBY ATTRACTIONS: Hendy Woods State Park (hiking, camping); Navarro River (swimming, fishing, wildlife viewing).

BRUTOCAO FAMILY VINEYARDS

BRUTOCAO FAMILY VINEYARDS ANDERSON VALLEY TASTING ROOM:
7000 Hwy. 128
Philo, CA 95466
800-661-2103

SCHOOLHOUSE PLAZA:
13500 U.S. 101
Hopland, CA 95449
800-433-3689
brutocao@pacific.net
www.brutocaocellars.com

OWNERS: Brutocao family.

LOCATIONS: Hwy. 128 in Anderson Valley; U.S. 101 in downtown Hopland.

APPELLATIONS: Anderson Valley, Mendocino.

HOURS: 10 A.M.–5 P.M. daily (both locations).

TASTINGS: Complimentary.

TOURS: By appointment (complimentary).

THE WINES: Barbera, Cabernet Sauvignon, Chardonnay, Dolcetto, Merlot, Pinot Noir, Port, Primitivo, Sangiovese, Sauvignon Blanc, Zinfandel.

SPECIALTIES: Italian varietals, Quadriga (Italian varietal blend).

WINEMAKER: Hoss Milone.

ANNUAL PRODUCTION: 15,000 cases.

OF SPECIAL NOTE: Hopland: Bocce courts. New on-site restaurant. Picnic areas with tables on shaded terraces. Annual events include Hopland Passport (May and October). Philo: Picnic area with tables and umbrellas under a shade arbor. Annual events include Anderson Valley Pinot Noir Festival (May). Port and reserve wines available only at tasting rooms.

NEARBY ATTRACTIONS: Hopland: Real Goods Solar Living Center (tours, store). Philo: Hendy Woods State Park (hiking, camping).

Brutocao Family Vineyards is a tale of two families who combined their skills and expertise to establish one of Mendocino County's most notable wineries. The Brutocaos immigrated from Venice in the early 1900s, bringing with them a passion for wine. Len Brutocao met Marty Bliss while in school at Berkeley. Marty's father, Irv, had been farming land in Mendocino since the 1940s. Len and Marty married, and soon thereafter the families joined forces and began to grow grapes. The family sold their grapes to other wineries for years before starting to make their own wine in 1991.

They selected the Lion of St. Mark from St. Mark's Cathedral in Venice as their symbol of family tradition and quality. The heart of that quality, they say, is in their 575 acres of vineyards in southern Mendocino County and another 11 acres of Pinot Noir in Anderson Valley.

Today, four generations of Brutocaos continue the family traditions, using estate grapes to produce a wide range of wines, including Italian varietals and blends. The wines are bottled under two labels: Brutocao Cellars, which focuses on premium vintages, and Bliss Family Vineyards, a new line of reasonably priced wines. The winery's first tasting room, a redwood building once occupied by another winery, is in Anderson Valley, site of the Brutocao family's eleven-acre cool-climate Pinot Noir vineyard. With its high-beamed ceilings, wisteria-covered patio, and umbrella-shaded picnic tables, it makes an ideal stop for those traveling scenic Highway 128 to the Pacific Coast.

In the late 1990s, the Brutocaos decided to open a second tasting room on U.S. 101. In 1997 they purchased the old Hopland High School from the Fetzer wine family and created a seven-and-a-half-acre complex, Schoolhouse Plaza, dedicated to food and wine. Both a tasting room and a restaurant are in the remodeled 1920s building, which still has its original facade bearing the high school's name. On display in the tasting room are memorabilia from the school's glory days. The complex also has a large conference room and a full-service bar. Visitors can sip a glass of wine while perusing the large gift shop or can dine alfresco overlooking the landscaped grounds, which include beautiful gardens of lavender, roses, and wildflowers.

The Brutocaos brought more than a love of food and wine when they came to this country. They are also passionate about bocce ball, a devilishly challenging game with a half-century Italian lineage. The Hopland complex has six regulation bocce ball courts, which are lighted and open to the public. Visitors can participate in friendly competitions free of charge or watch the games as they relax on terraces or the expanse of manicured lawn with a peaked-roof gazebo.

DREW FAMILY CELLARS

On its journey from mountains to the sea, Highway 128 passes through the quaint village of Philo, in the heart of the pastoral Anderson Valley. At the southern edge of town, a tall sign beckons travelers to "taste, shop, and relax" at the Madrones, a collection of tasting rooms and shops. The Drew Family Cellars tasting room occupies a cozy space within the Spanish-Mediterranean complex. On the walls hang photos of a young couple and their two children picking apples and stomping grapes at a rural vineyard estate. Given the couple's youthful appearance, one might assume that the Drews are relative newcomers in the winemaking business. But Jason Drew is no neophyte in the world of wine. He has journeyed through it for more than two decades, culminating today with wide acclaim for his restrained, balanced style of making Pinot Noir.

Jason Drew's interest in growing grapes and making wine began as a teenager, when he helped out at his uncle's six-acre vineyard in Napa Valley. He majored in agricultural ecology and viticulture at the University of California, Santa Cruz, then worked as an intern at St. Supéry Winery in Napa and as a vineyard manager at Carmenet Winery in Sonoma. His wife, Molly, shared his passion for working with the land. The couple moved to Mendocino County, where Jason managed and developed vineyards for Navarro Vineyards. Around this time, his experiences working alongside world-class vintners inspired him to become a winemaker. He and Molly went to Australia, where Jason earned a graduate enology degree at the University of Adelaide. After their return to California in 1998, he worked at several well-known wineries, including Babcock Vineyards in the Sta. Rita Hills AVA, famed for its Pinot Noirs.

All these early experiences laid the foundation for the next stage of the Drews' journey: their own winery and biodynamic vineyard. They searched for a cool-climate site where soils were conducive to making exceptional Pinot Noir. In 2004 they bought a twenty-six-acre apple orchard in the Mendocino Ridge AVA and planted seven acres of Pinot Noir vines. The Drews consider the property a new frontier—it's the closest vineyard in Mendocino County to the Pacific Ocean, which is just three miles west. But it sits on a sunny ridge at 1,250 feet above sea level, well above the fog line. The Drews built a new winery, which includes their private residence on the second floor. Here Jason crafts six different Pinot Noirs and a cool-climate Syrah each year, using grapes sourced from various local vineyards. The family looks forward to the first harvest of their own estate grapes in 2014.

DREW FAMILY CELLARS
9000 Hwy. 128
Philo, CA 95466
707-895-9599
info@drewwines.com
www.drewwines.com

OWNERS: Jason and Molly Drew.

LOCATION: The Madrones, at southern edge of Philo.

APPELLATIONS: Mendocino Ridge, Anderson Valley, Yorkville Highlands.

HOURS: 11 A.M.–5 P.M. Thursday–Monday in winter and spring, also Wednesdays in summer and fall.

TASTINGS: $5 for 4 wines.

TOURS: None.

THE WINES: Albariño, Pinot Noir, Syrah.

SPECIALTIES: Small-lot vineyard-designated and appellation-specific wines, with a main focus on Pinot Noir and cool-climate Syrah.

WINEMAKER: Jason Drew.

ANNUAL PRODUCTION: 1,700 cases.

OF SPECIAL NOTE: Wines available only in tasting room. Wines available for purchase by the glass. Annual events include Anderson Valley Pinot Noir Festival (May). Deli items sold at adjacent shop. Shaded arcade and courtyard with tables. Two suites and two apartments for rent at the Madrones.

NEARBY ATTRACTIONS: Hendy Woods State Park (hiking, camping); Navarro River (swimming, fishing, wildlife viewing).

JERIKO ESTATE

JERIKO ESTATE
12141 Hewlitt and
Sturtevant Rd.
Hopland, CA 95449
707-744-1140
info@jerikoestate.com
www.jerikoestate.com

OWNER: Daniel Fetzer.

LOCATION: About 2 miles
north of Hopland via
U.S. 101.

APPELLATION: Mendocino.

HOURS: 10 A.M.–5 P.M. daily.

TASTINGS: $8.50 for flights
of 6, or by the glass.

TOURS: By appointment.

THE WINES: Chardonnay,
Pinot Noir, Sangiovese,
Sauvignon Blanc, Syrah.

SPECIALTIES: *Méthode
champenoise* Brut and
Pinot Noir.

WINEMAKER: Cesar Toxqui.

ANNUAL PRODUCTION:
25,000 cases.

OF SPECIAL NOTE: Several
picnic sites around the
estate; gourmet food
products available in
tasting room. Annual
events include Hopland
Passport Weekend (May
and October). Brut Rosé,
Grenache Noir, and
Sauvignon Blanc available
only in tasting room.

NEARBY ATTRACTIONS:
Grace Hudson House
(museum of art, history,
and anthropology); Held-
Poage Memorial Home
and Research Library
(Mendocino County
history); Real Goods
Solar Living Center
(tours, store).

The Fetzer family has been a major force in Mendocino County winemaking for decades, ever since Barney and Kathleen Fetzer produced their first commercial wine vintage in 1968 from grapes grown on an estate they had bought ten years earlier. The family is also acclaimed for having pioneered organic grape growing in California.

Skip forward to 1997, when Daniel Fetzer, Barney and Kathleen's son, began planting Pinot Noir, Chardonnay, Syrah, Merlot, Sauvignon Blanc, and Sangiovese grapes on his own 200-acre ranch just north of Hopland. Now, he farms 120 acres of estate vineyards that extend from the foothills eastward, all the way across U.S. 101 to the Russian River. Staying true to his family heritage in another way, Fetzer uses organic and biodynamic farming techniques. He released his first vintage, a Chardonnay, in 2000, but his most precious claim to fame is the distinction of having produced the county's first organic sparkling wine, a Brut, in 2001.

Fetzer decided to name his winery Jeriko Estate, evoking the ancient city of Jeriko in the region where plants and animals were first domesticated (also known as "the city of agriculture"). Visitors approach the winery through a series of formidable iron gates that Fetzer embellished with crests and flanked with imposing stone columns of his own design. The view from the road offers a panoramic display of early California and Mediterranean-style architecture expressed in dun-colored, low-rise buildings topped with red tile roofs. Irregularly spaced, statuesque Canary Island date palms punctuate the Mediterranean influence. Olive trees have been planted around the visitor center. In front of the entrance, low stone walls surround a manicured field of grass divided into quadrangles in the formal Italian style. Sheep, goats, and horses can often be seen grazing around the vineyards closest to the winery, and ducks and other wildlife frequent the estate's ponds.

Behind the winemaking facility stands the original estate residence, built in 1898 by San Francisco Judge J. H. Sturtevant. Daniel Fetzer extensively redesigned the structure a century later for use as a hospitality center for VIPs. The home's color scheme provided the inspiration for the adjacent winery and visitor center, constructed in 1999. Inside the center, soaring glass walls enclose the enormous barrel room where stack after stack of aging wine is easily visible from every angle. Also on display is a casual exhibit of historic winemaking equipment, including an antique French riddling rack once used in the production of *méthode champenoise* sparkling wines. In a corner near the tasting bar, a pair of comfortably worn leather sofas are arranged in a conversational grouping in front of a giant fireplace.

PARDUCCI WINE CELLARS

The roots of Parducci Wine Cellars—the oldest winery in Mendocino County—run deep. Adolph and Isabel Parducci moved from Tuscany to California in 1912 and bought a vineyard in the hills above the Ukiah Valley in 1921. They and their four sons built a winery with tanks made of huge old-growth redwood and began legally making wine in 1932, at the end of the Prohibition era. Visitors tasted Parducci wines, including the signature Petite Sirah (the winery was the first in the state to label this varietal), in the cellar beneath the family's home.

Today's Parducci Wine Cellars, while reflecting many of its historic traditions, has a completely different program. The Parduccis sold the winery and Home Ranch estate in 1996. The Thornhill family acquired the property  in 2004, and three generations of Thornhills now live and work here, including brothers Tim and Tom. Tim Thornhill, a successful landscape architect, is passionate about organic and sustainable living. He and his relatives immediately launched plans to create a model culture of sustainability.

Head winemaker Bob Swain has crafted wine for Parducci Wine Cellars since 1997. He also oversees the estate vineyards and helps manage the winery's relationships with ten to fifteen growers, many of whom have farmed the same vineyard blocks and sold the fruit to Parducci for generations. These vineyards, scattered throughout Mendocino County, reflect the region's incredible diversity of slopes, soils, elevations, and microclimates. The winery enjoys an enviable position of access to a wide range of grapes, grown in small blocks at various sites, for example, on sunny hilltops above the fog line (ideal for ripening Zinfandel and Cabernet Sauvignon), and in cool-climate Anderson Valley and along the Russian River, where Chardonnay and Pinot Noir typically develop rich complexity and character.

Swain likes to call this broad access to diverse fruit "the winemaker's spice rack." He takes special advantage of it when making the winery's artisanal Small Lot Blend wines. The diversity gives him great flexibility, and knowledge of each vineyard block's particular attributes helps him choose the best varietals for each blend.

Visitors sample Parducci wines in the Spanish-Mediterranean tasting room, built and furnished using recycled bricks, pine, and redwood. For a dose of Parducci history, guests should request a tour of the original winery, which holds seventy-eight old-growth redwood tanks, some a century old, and the Cellar House, the original family tasting room with historical photos, where the Parduccis poured their wines for many years.

PARDUCCI WINE CELLARS
501 Parducci Rd.
Ukiah, CA 95482
888-362-9463
tasting@parducci.com
www.parducci.com

OWNERS:
Thomas A. Thornhill III,
Tim Thornhill,
Tommy Thornhill Jr.

LOCATION: 5 miles north of Ukiah via Lake Mendocino Dr. exit off Hwy. 101.

APPELLATION: Mendocino.

HOURS: 10 A.M.–5 P.M. daily.

TASTINGS: $5 for 4 wines.

TOURS: Complimentary guided tours of winery and/or wetlands on request, subject to staff availability.

THE WINES: Cabernet Sauvignon, Chardonnay, Merlot, Petite Sirah, Pinot Gris, Pinot Noir, Sauvignon Blanc, Zinfandel.

SPECIALTIES: Small Lot Blend Pinot Noir and True Grit Reserve Cabernet Sauvignon.

WINEMAKER: Bob Swain.

ANNUAL PRODUCTION: 80,000 cases.

OF SPECIAL NOTE: Restored wetlands that support wildlife. Patios with picnic areas. Well-stocked gift shop with eclectic gifts and small selection of cheeses, sandwiches, and lunch items from local restaurants. Acoustic Café concerts June–September. Annual events include Death by Chocolate (February), Holiday Celebration (December), and Murder Mystery Dinners. Estate-grown reserve wines available only in tasting room.

NEARBY ATTRACTIONS: Real Goods Solar Living Center (tours, store); Lake Mendocino (hiking, boating, fishing, camping).

ROEDERER ESTATE

ROEDERER ESTATE
4501 Hwy. 128
Philo, CA 95466
707-895-2288 ext. 22
info@roedererestate.com
www.roedererestate.com

OWNER: Champagne Louis Roederer.

LOCATION: 5 miles northwest of Philo.

APPELLATION: Anderson Valley.

HOURS: 11 A.M.–5 P.M. daily.

TASTINGS: $6 for 8 wines.

TOURS: Guided tours ($6 per person) by appointment.

THE WINES: Chardonnay, Pinot Noir.

SPECIALTIES: Sparkling wines made from estate grapes using *méthode champenoise*.

WINEMAKER: Arnaud Weyrich.

ANNUAL PRODUCTION: 100,000 cases.

OF SPECIAL NOTE: Picnic lunches for two ($25) available upon arrival with advance reservation. Patio and lawn; picnic tables with umbrellas. Winery is pet friendly. Annual events include the International Alsace Varietals Festival (February), Anderson Valley Pinot Noir Festival (May), and Patio Festival (July). Wines available only in tasting room include library wines, Extra Dry sparkling wine, Chardonnay, Pinot Noir, and Rosé of Pinot Noir.

NEARBY ATTRACTIONS: Hendy Woods State Park (hiking, camping); Navarro River (swimming, fishing, wildlife viewing).

Famed French sparkling wine house Champagne Louis Roederer has been making classic European-style bottles of bubbly for nearly two hundred years. In the early 1980s, Jean-Claude Rouzaud, a fifth-generation descendant of the founder, visited California to search for suitable land on which to establish a New World wine estate. The state's cool-climate regions caught his attention, as he felt that the varied microclimates and long growing season held great potential to produce grapes ideally suited to Roederer's winemaking style, known for its body, finesse, and depth of flavor. In 1982 he discovered an ideal property: 580 acres at the northwestern edge of the Anderson Valley.

Since the beginning, Roederer Estate has focused on two essential elements that have served the company well. First, only estate-grown grapes are used to make wines in Roederer's own facility, to maintain total control of the vineyard and winemaking process from start to finish. Roederer now has 600 acres of Pinot Noir and Chardonnay (including 120 acres at sister winery Scharffenberger Cellars in Philo, five miles east). All estate vineyards are farmed sustainably, including 90 organic acres and 22 biodynamic acres. Second, Roederer makes a "secret ingredient"—its own reserve wines, aged in French oak casks for three to five years in a separate cellar, to add to each blend, or cuvée. Few, if any, wineries in the world make sparkling wines with reserves aged this long, which increase depth and complexity in the blend.

Although the techniques are those used in Europe, winemaker Arnaud Weyrich crafts wines that express a decidedly Californian character emanating from the grapes' Mendocino County *terroir*. Signature vintages include the Brut and Brut Rosé, both multivintage blends of Chardonnay and Pinot Noir. L'Ermitage and L'Ermitage Rosé are the winery's prestige cuvées: sparkling wines made only in exceptional years with grapes from the estate's finest vineyards plus a trace amount of reserve wines. The winery also produces small amounts of still wines: Pinot Noir, Chardonnay, and Rosé of Pinot Noir.

Visitors taste these wines at the estate's winery and visitor center, a rustic redwood building perched on a hilltop. Sweeping views of the Anderson Valley unfold from expansive lawn, terrace, and gardens—ideal spots for lingering over a glass of sparkling wine and a picnic at umbrella-shaded tables. Indoors, guests enjoy sparkling wine pours from magnums (a rare opportunity) and bottles at a black walnut bar. The spacious room is filled with French antiques and casual furnishings one might find in a local resident's home. A series of twelve historic woodcuts depicting the traditional French *méthode champenoise* winemaking process is a reminder of the estate's two-century pedigree.

SCHARFFENBERGER CELLARS

Life in the tiny Anderson Valley town of Philo hasn't changed much since its pioneer era in the mid-1800s. Residents stroll along quiet streets to Philo's center, a half-mile stretch of services along Highway 128, to fetch the mail, pick up supplies at the local market, and chat with friends over coffee on a porch. Scharffenberger Cellars estate vineyards occupy 120 acres in the heart of town; its tasting room, in a former 1950s home right on Highway 128, connects visitors with the essence of the Philo wine country experience. Outdoors, guests can enjoy wines by the glass and watch the slow parade of Philo life pass by, while sitting at tables on a shaded veranda or in two garden areas.

Indoors, they view exhibits of local art on their way back to the tasting bar, a unique glass-topped composite of small pieces of wine bottles, sea urchin spines, and cop-per flecks, made by a local artist. Here they sample a range of premium sparkling wines — Scharffenberger Cellars' specialty — and a handful of still wines, all made from estate and Mendocino County grapes.

The winery, on the site of an 1850s homestead, first opened in 1981. John Scharffenberger bought it in 1992 and founded Scharffenberger Cellars. He designed the winery label himself — an old-world-style family crest with two dancing bears. The bear is the official symbol of the state of California, and the bears' appearance illustrates the winery's California style of making sparkling wine: softer, fruitier, and less acidic than its European counterparts. Winemaker Tex Sawyer has been crafting Scharffenberger Cellars wines since 1989. His most popular sparkling wines include the Brut NV and the Rosé NV, both produced with varying percentages of Pinot Noir and Chardonnay. He also makes sparkling Blanc de Blanc (all Chardonnay), Crémant (Pinot Noir and Chardonnay), and Extra Dry (similar to the Brut but sweeter), plus very small lots of Chardonnay and Pinot Noir.

Many visitors ask if Scharffenberger Cellars is related to Scharffen Berger chocolate. The answer is yes…and no. John Scharffenberger sold his eponymous winery in 1995, along with the rights to the name. He later launched his chocolate business, but had to alter the name to avoid trademark issues. The winery experienced a series of ownerships and name changes until Champagne Louis Roederer bought it in 2003 and reinstated the Scharffenberger Cellars designation. Sister winery Roederer Estate, also renowned for sparkling wines, lies five miles west of Philo. Although John Scharffenberger is no longer officially associated with the winery and vineyards, visitors can purchase bars of Scharffen Berger chocolate, as well as gifts and sundries, many created by residents of Philo, Anderson Valley, and the Mendocino County region.

SCHARFFENBERGER CELLARS
8501 Hwy. 128
Philo, CA 95466
707-895-2957
info@scharffenbergercellars.com
www.scharffenbergercellars.com

OWNER: Champagne Louis Roederer.

LOCATION: In the town of Philo, on Highway 128.

APPELLATION: Anderson Valley.

HOURS: 11 A.M.–5 P.M. daily.

TASTINGS: $3 for 10 wines.

TOURS: By appointment.

THE WINES: Chardonnay, Pinot Noir.

SPECIALTY: Sparkling wine.

WINEMAKER: Tex Sawyer.

ANNUAL PRODUCTION: 25,000 cases.

OF SPECIAL NOTE: Picnic tables on shaded porch and covered patio, and in garden areas. Picnic lunches ($25) delivered upon arrival with advance reservation. Revolving art exhibits, with opening receptions for new shows every three months. Well-stocked gift shop with local and regional items. Formal and casual gardens. Winery is pet friendly. Wines available only in tasting room include Blanc de Blanc, Crémant, and Extra Dry sparkling wines, and Chardonnay, Pinot Noir, and Syrah. Annual events include International Alsace Varietals Festival (February) and Anderson Valley Pinot Noir Festival (May).

NEARBY ATTRACTIONS: Hendy Woods State Park (hiking, camping); Navarro River (swimming, fishing, wildlife viewing).

SEEBASS VINEYARDS AND FAMILY WINES

SEEBASS VINEYARDS AND FAMILY WINES
3300 Old River Rd.
Ukiah, CA 95482
707-467-9463
info@seebassvineyards.com
www.seebassvineyards.com

OWNER: Brigitte Seebass.

LOCATION: 2 miles southeast of downtown Ukiah.

APPELLATION: Mendocino.

HOURS: 11 A.M.–5 P.M. Friday–Sunday and by appointment.

TASTINGS: $3 for up to 5 wines.

TOURS: Complimentary guided tours by appointment and special tours throughout the year.

THE WINES: Chardonnay, Grenache, Syrah, Zinfandel.

SPECIALTIES: Wines from estate-grown fruit.

WINEMAKERS: Stepháne Vivier and Greg Graziano.

ANNUAL PRODUCTION: 2,500 cases.

OF SPECIAL NOTE: Picnic area by a pond. Century-old Zinfandel vines. Winery is pet friendly. All wines available only in tasting room.

NEARBY ATTRACTIONS: Real Goods Solar Living Center (tours, store); Lake Mendocino (hiking, boating, fishing, camping); Grace Hudson Museum (Pomo Indian baskets, historical photographs, changing art exhibits); Vichy Springs (mineral springs and resort).

In the 1980s, only a handful of wineries existed in Mendocino County. Compared to neighboring Napa and Sonoma, the area was still relatively undiscovered. Brigitte Seebass arrived on this nascent scene in 1988, lured by the excellent investment opportunities and the chance to be part of an up-and-coming wine region. She became Mendocino's first female vineyard owner when she purchased a hundred-acre property with eight acres of century-old Zinfandel vines on the gentle slopes of the Russian River Valley east of Ukiah.

Seebass's love of the land and zeal for new beginnings stem from her fascinating heritage. For more than eight centuries, the extended Seebass family had farmed land in Saxony and Bavaria in southern Germany. A local friar drew the first known family crest, in 1363, which appears on the winery's labels. Brigitte Seebass was born and raised on a Saxon farm in the 1940s. As a teenager, she found herself about to be trapped behind the Iron Curtain and escaped to the West via train, eventually making her way to London, where she met her future husband. In 1968 they moved to California's Silicon Valley, where daughter Michelle was born.

After Seebass purchased the 106-acre Talmage property in 1988, she kept the old vine Zinfandel section of the vineyard and over the next four years replanted eighty-eight acres to Chardonnay, Syrah, Grenache, and Merlot. Until recently, Seebass Vineyards sold nearly all its grapes, lauded for their consistent quality, to major wineries. Every two to three years, Seebass held back two tons of grapes to make wines strictly for family consumption, calling upon local Greg Graziano, former winemaker at La Crema, to produce the vintages. In 2009 she began to pass the reins to daughter Michelle and her husband, Scott. The business name was changed to Seebass Vineyards and Family Wines to reflect their plans to share with the public their wines previously reserved for the family. Greg Graziano continues to oversee Chardonnay, Zinfandel, and blended wine production, and Napa-based Stepháne Vivier crafts French-style Chardonnay, Syrah, and Merlot. The winery offers three red wines—Old Vine Zinfandel, Syrah, and Mysteriös (a blend of Grenache, Syrah, and Merlot)—and two Chardonnays, one a French-style wine, the other a lighter, bolder Italian version.

Visitors to the estate on Old River Road can tour the pristine grounds, which include an olive tree–lined pond that attracts waterfowl and other wildlife. Samples of Seebass wines are poured in a tiny tasting room in a converted farm building on the edge of the vineyard, a short walk from the family home and organic gardens. A reflection of the Seebass family's long tradition of land, food, and wine hangs on the wall—the regal crest drawn by the family friar in Bavaria in 1363.

ACKNOWLEDGMENTS

Creativity, perseverance, integrity, and commitment are fundamental qualities
for guaranteeing the success of a project. The artistic and editorial teams who worked on
this edition possess these qualities in large measures. My heartfelt thanks go to K. Reka Badger,
Cheryl Crabtree, and Marty Olmstead, writers; Robert Holmes, photographer;
Judith Dunham, copyeditor; Linda Bouchard, proofreader; Poulson Gluck Design, production;
Scott Runcorn, color correction; and Ben Pease, cartographer.

In addition, I am grateful for the invaluable counsel and encouragement of Chester and
Frances Arnold; Greg Taylor; my esteemed parents — Estelle Silberkleit and William Silberkleit;
Danny Biederman; and the scores of readers and winery enthusiasts who have contacted me
over the past decade to say how much they enjoy this book series.

I also extend my deepest appreciation to Ann Everett-Cotroneo and the staff of the Hampton Inn
in the town of Ukiah for their excellent hospitality and enthusiastic support of this project.
And finally, for her love and creative input, as well as for enduring work-filled weekends
and midnight deadlines, my gratitude and affection go to Lisa Silberkleit.

— Tom Silberkleit

OTHER BOOKS BY WINE HOUSE PRESS

The California Directory of Fine Wineries — Central Coast
Santa Barbara • San Luis Obispo • Paso Robles

Wine House Press
127 East Napa Street, Suite E, Sonoma, CA 95476
707-996-1741

Editor and publisher: Tom Silberkleit
Original design: Jennifer Barry Design
Production: Poulson Gluck Design
Copyeditor: Judith Dunham
Cartographer: Ben Pease
Color correction: Eviltron
Artistic development: Lisa Silberkleit
Proofreader: Linda Bouchard

All photographs by Robert Holmes, except the following:
page 32, bottom left: Paul Kirchner; page 101, bottom left: Damon Mattson; page 114, bottom left: Duncan Garrett;
page 115: Avis Mandel; page 127: Peter Griffith Photography; page 133, bottom left: Timm Eubanks.

Front cover photograph: Vineyards in Los Carneros, Napa, CA
Back cover photographs: top left: Beringer Vineyards; top right: Mumm Napa;
bottom left: Swanson Vineyards; bottom right: Rutherford Hill Winery.

Printed and bound in Singapore through Imago Sales (USA) Inc.
ISBN-13: 978-0-9724993-9-2

Sixth Edition

Distributed by Publishers Group West, 1700 Fourth Street, Berkeley, CA 94710, www.pgw.com

The publisher has made every effort to ensure the accuracy of the information contained in
The California Directory of Fine Wineries, but can accept no liability for any loss, injury, or inconvenience
sustained by any visitor as a result of any information or recommendation contained in this guide.
Travelers should always call ahead to confirm hours of operation, fees, and other highly variable information.

Always act responsibly when drinking alcoholic beverages by selecting a designated driver or prearranged transportation.

Customized Editions
Wine House Press will print custom editions of this volume for bulk purchase at your request. Personalized covers and
foil-stamped corporate logo imprints can be created in large quantities for special promotions or events, or as premiums.
For more information, contact Custom Imprints, Wine House Press, 127 E. Napa Street, Suite E, Sonoma, CA 95476; 707-996-1741.

Join the Facebook Fan Page: www.facebook.com/CaliforniaFineWineries
Follow us on Twitter: twitter.com/cafinewineries
Scan to visit our website: www.CaliforniaFineWineries.com